S0-EIC-123

Classroom Scenes and Monologues

Compiled and Edited

by

KENT R. BROWN

Dramatic Publishing
Woodstock, Illinois • England • Australia • New Zealand

*** NOTICE ***

Professionals and amateurs are hereby warned that each scene and monologue in this book is fully protected under the copyright laws of the United States of America, the British Commonwealth, including Canada, and all other countries of the Copyright Union. Scenes and monologues may be used for audition purposes only without royalty; however, all scenes and monologues in this volume are subject to royalty payment for: professional and amateur performances, motion pictures, lecturing, public readings, radio broadcasting, television, reprinting, and translation into foreign languages.

For royalty information and permission to perform, other than auditions, please refer to the permission acknowledgment pages at the end of this book to locate the source able to grant permission for public performance. The permission acknowledgment section constitutes an extension of this copyright page.

Published by The Dramatic Publishing Company
P.O. Box 129, Woodstock IL 60098
www.dramaticpublishing.com

For performance of any songs, music and recordings mentioned in this book which are in copyright, the permission of the copyright owners must be obtained or other songs and recordings in the public domain substituted.

©MMV by
KENT R. BROWN

Printed in the United States of America
All Rights Reserved
(CLASSROOM SCENES AND MONOLOGUES)

ISBN: 1-58342-281-1

CONTENTS

CLASSROOM SCENES

CLASSROOM MONOLOGUES

CLASSROOM SCENES

BEST FRIENDS
A Dilemma in Dueling Monologues
By Sandra Fenichel Asher

CHARACTERS

SOPHIE: A teenager, Megan's best friend
MEGAN: A teenager, Sophie's best friend

TIME: The present.

PLACE: A teenage girl's bedroom, but somewhat stylized because the one space represents both Sophie's and Megan's rooms in different houses. On the right: a bed, bedside table with phone, and bookcase. On the left: a chest of drawers, desk and chairs. Pillows, stuffed animals, and photos on both sides, but the right side is neatly arranged, while the left is a jumble of shoes, clothes, bookbag, books, snacks and other debris.

MEGAN and SOPHIE move about the space unaware of one another, as if they were in separate rooms. Whenever MEGAN moves from one side to the other, she tidies up. Whenever SOPHIE moves from one side to the other, she's unable to find whatever she's looking for at the moment and creates a new mess searching for it. The girls do their tidying and searching nonchalantly, almost unconsciously, a metaphor for the many ways friends adjust to and accommodate one another's habits and idiosyncracies.

AT RISE: *MUSIC. MEGAN is at right, making the bed, arranging pillows and stuffed toys, tucking a notebook and pen into the bedside table drawer, rearranging the bookshelves neatly. SOPHIE is at left, searching for her history textbook by emptying her bookbag and most of her bureau and desk drawers onto the floor. As they continue these activities, the girls speak to the audience as if to a visiting friend. MUSIC fades.*

SOPHIE. Megan is my best friend.

MEGAN. Sophie is my best friend.

SOPHIE. We've known each other forever.

MEGAN. I can't remember a time when we *weren't* best friends.

SOPHIE. She's always lived next door.

MEGAN. We met through the chain-link fence between our back yards.

SOPHIE. We used to play in her sandbox.

MEGAN. We used to play on her swing set.

SOPHIE. Our moms swear we started out speaking gibberish to one another before we even learned how to talk.

MEGAN. Our moms swear we still speak gibberish to one another, the way we did then.

(MUSIC. Unable to find her history book anywhere on her messy side of the room, SOPHIE crosses right, where she begins emptying the bookshelves onto the floor looking for it. At last, she finds it, grabs the notebook and pen out of the bedside table, unmakes the bed, hops in, arranges pillows and stuffed toys or tosses them on the floor until she's comfortable. At the same time, satisfied that her side of the room is in or-

der, MEGAN crosses left and begins tidying up the mess left behind by SOPHIE. MUSIC fades. Activity continues as they speak.)

MEGAN. It's unbelievable how much we have in common.

SOPHIE. People sometimes think we're sisters.

MEGAN. We're practically twins.

SOPHIE. Which is weird, because we really don't look alike at all.

MEGAN. We like the same music.

SOPHIE. We like the same movies.

MEGAN. We like the same clothes.

SOPHIE. We like the same boys... *(Suddenly, her mood grows dark. She abruptly stops talking and busies herself with her notebook and pen.)*

MEGAN. We like the same *boy*... *(Just as suddenly, her mood darkens and she begins stuffing and slamming drawers angrily instead of in her usual calm and orderly manner.)*

SOPHIE *(after a moment of furious scribbling)*. Of course, we're not *totally* alike.

MEGAN *(after a moment of furious stuffing)*. We're really very different.

SOPHIE. Ask anyone—our friends, our teachers, our families.

MEGAN. People mention it all the time.

SOPHIE *(mockingly)*. "Megan's the pretty one."

MEGAN *(mockingly)*. "Sophie's got those eyes! Sophie's got that hair!"

SOPHIE *(mockingly)*. "Megan's the smart one."

MEGAN *(mockingly)*. "Sophie aced the exam! Sophie got straight A's!"

SOPHIE. She leads. I follow.
MEGAN. She leads. I follow.
SOPHIE. That's what everyone says.
MEGAN. Ask anyone at all.
SOPHIE. Only they're *wrong!*

(*MUSIC. Finished tidying up at left, MEGAN crosses right and begins straightening the bookshelves again. She remakes the bed, rearranges the pillows and toys, and sits on the edge of the bed, hugging a favorite stuffed animal. At the same time, SOPHIE hops out of bed, crosses left, and begins another messy search, this time for her hairbrush, which she eventually locates. She brushes her hair vigorously. MUSIC fades. Activities continue under dialogue.*)

SOPHIE. I saw him *first.*
MEGAN. *I* saw him first.
SOPHIE (*transported back to the fateful moment*). He *smiled* at me.
MEGAN (*transported back to the fateful moment*). He smiled at *me.*
SOPHIE. And I told her—
MEGAN. I told her—
SOPHIE. "Look at him!"
MEGAN. "He's gorgeous!"
SOPHIE. "Who is he?"
MEGAN. "Isn't that Meredith's cousin?"
SOPHIE. "He must be Meredith's cousin!"
MEGAN. "He just moved here."
SOPHIE. "He just moved here from New York."
MEGAN. "Andrew! Isn't that his name?"
SOPHIE. "Andrew! That's it! His name is Andrew!"

MEGAN. "Wow!"

SOPHIE. "Wow!"

MEGAN. "Wow!"

SOPHIE. "Wow!"

MEGAN *(back in the present, talking to unseen friend, relishing the memory)*. He *danced* with me.

SOPHIE *(back in the present, talking to unseen friend, relishing the memory)*. He danced with *me*.

MEGAN. Twice!

SOPHIE. He danced with Megan first. But then he danced with me!

MEGAN *(drooping)*. He called Sophie to get the history assignment.

SOPHIE *(drooping)*. He sat next to *her* in the library.

MEGAN. What if he calls her again?

SOPHIE. What if he likes her best?

MEGAN. It isn't fair!

SOPHIE. I saw him first!

(MUSIC. MEGAN crosses left and tidies up more slowly now, thinking things over. SOPHIE crosses right, hops onto bed, gathers several stuffed animals close for comfort, thinking things over. MUSIC fades.)

MEGAN. I know she really likes him. I can tell.

SOPHIE. She likes him. A lot. I can tell.

MEGAN. But I liked him *first!*

SOPHIE. I like him *more!*

MEGAN. Maybe I should say something to her.

SOPHIE. Maybe I should let her know.

MEGAN. But what would that change?

SOPHIE. What could she do?

MEGAN. If she likes him, she likes him.

SOPHIE. If he likes her, he likes her.

MEGAN. And I'll just drink some Liquid-Plumr.

SOPHIE. And I'll curl up and die.

(*MUSIC. Another cross. This time SOPHIE is looking for her cell phone. MEGAN goes to the bedside phone, lifts the receiver, replaces it, stares at it glumly. MUSIC fades. Activity continues.*)

MEGAN. We need to talk about this.

SOPHIE. I wish we could talk.

MEGAN. But what's the use?

SOPHIE. My head's in a muddle.

MEGAN. It'd all come out gibberish.

SOPHIE. Megan would understand.

MEGAN. If only we could talk.

SOPHIE. She always understands.

MEGAN. But how can we talk about *this?*

SOPHIE (*finds her phone, but doesn't dial*). What if she gets mad?

MEGAN (*reaches for receiver, but doesn't lift it*). What if she stops speaking to me?

SOPHIE. What if she ends up hating me?

MEGAN. What if they *both* end up hating me?

SOPHIE. I'll just drink some Liquid-Plumr.

MEGAN. I'll curl up and die!

SOPHIE (*another hesitant glance at the phone*). I don't know what to *do.*

MEGAN (*another hesitant glance at the phone*). I don't know what to *say.*

SOPHIE. Megan is my *best friend.*

MEGAN. Sophie is my *best friend.*

(MUSIC. SOPHIE turns the cell phone on—punches in the first five digits of MEGAN's phone number, the first three quickly, the next two with growing hesitation. At the exact same time and in the same rhythm, MEGAN lifts the receiver of her phone and punches in the first five digits of SOPHIE's number. After the fifth digit, BOTH stop short, overcome by doubt. A beat, and then BOTH hang up. They freeze, caught up in their mutual dilemma. LIGHTS fade. MUSIC fades.)

BLACKOUT

HANDS
By Max Bush

<u>CHARACTERS</u>

KYLE: 18.
ABBY: Early 20s, homeless.

TIME: Saturday noon.
PLACE: A park; bench, tree, rows of bushes.

AT RISE: *KYLE is seated on the park bench. He is rest-*
ing, thinking. ABBY enters and sees KYLE who does
not see her. She moves into his line of sight. Their eyes
meet.

ABBY. Ha! There!
KYLE. Hi.
ABBY. You trying to hide?
KYLE. Yes I am. But you found me.
ABBY. Why are you looking at me? *(He turns away.)*
  Why were you looking at me?
KYLE. It's all right, I was just looking to see if I knew
  you.
ABBY. Do you know me?
KYLE. I don't think so.
ABBY. Then you don't know much, yet.
KYLE *(giving up to ABBY; he can't escape now, so he*
  might as well make the best of it. Pleasantly). I've seen
  you before. What's your name?

ABBY *(takes out a child's beach shovel, points it at him).* Don't look at me. I don't want your diseases; I don't want your big ideas in my head, *(He looks away.)* and I don't want you to ignore me. I hate that. Being ignored. *(He looks back at her.)* Like I don't think; like I'm not here. Like I can't see. Like I can't see Las Vegas from here. I can see. I can see into your brain. I can take the pictures from your head and give them to the police.

KYLE. Wow. Can you show me the pictures first so I know what's going on in there?

ABBY. What are you talking about?

KYLE. Why are you talking to me and not other people in the park?

ABBY. I told you. Because I see pictures in your brain. You could love me. *(ABBY moves behind a tree or a bush, uses the child's shovel to dig something out of the ground. KYLE moves to watch her. She stands with a small box, a ring box. She opens it.)* A ring. A lost ring. Someone's life buried in the ring box. Someone's whole life around and around in the ring. Around and around and then it broke. *(She puts ring on.)* Bury it so the earth would make a path to it. He could come here on the path. He could find me. *(Suddenly very sad.)* I'm sorry. I couldn't help it. I didn't know. When you were shining I was on the other street. When you were bleeding, I heard you call but I couldn't find you. You're the one. You're the one, baby. Baby, my baby. You're the only one. Hands...your hands...I love your hands...put your hands on me, again. *(She takes out a clean, expensive, embroidered woman's handkerchief, wipes her eyes.)* I'm all...sorry. *(She dabs her eyes, carefully folds up her handkerchief, puts it away. She puts ring in box. She is, just as suddenly, no longer sad.)* Were you listening?

KYLE. No, I wasn't listening.

ABBY. Then why was I talking?

KYLE. I thought you were talking to yourself.

ABBY. Were you watching?

KYLE. No.

ABBY. Then why was I here?

KYLE. You told me not to look at you.

ABBY. You don't listen.

KYLE. I heard that. You told me I don't listen. So you see? I do listen.

ABBY. Listen to me, don't listen to me, ignore me, here I am, what the hell do you care.

KYLE. I do care.

ABBY. Ha! You see? I was right! That's why I'm talking to you. I wanted to look for you today, and here you are. Are you here?

KYLE. I'm here.

ABBY. You're waiting?

KYLE. Yeah, I'm waiting.

ABBY. Then I found you. *(Pause. She thinks, smiles.)* Congratulations!

KYLE. For what?

ABBY *(her smile vanishes)*. Bad manners.

KYLE. I have bad manners?

ABBY. I said something good to you and you didn't hear me.

KYLE. What did you say?

ABBY. I like your hands.

KYLE. Oh. Thank you.

ABBY *(waits, then)*. Well?

KYLE. What?

ABBY. What are you doing?

KYLE. I'm trying to talk to you but I don't seem to very good at it. Why did you want to find me? What do you want to say?

ABBY. You have bad manners.

KYLE. All right. I have bad manners. *(Silence. She waits. He sees she's waiting for something from him.)* I like your eyes. You can see Las Vegas from here. *(Silence. She continues to look at him expectantly.)*

ABBY. Well?

KYLE. I didn't hear you say anything.

ABBY *(formally)*. I simply couldn't speak any further with you without being invited to join you. May I?
(He smiles at her. He clears an area. She sits.)

KYLE. Oh. Of course. Please sit down.

ABBY. Thank you. *(Pleasantly, formally.)* Isn't it a lovely day?

KYLE. Yeah.

ABBY. How are you?

KYLE. A little confused, but it's cool you're sitting here with me.

ABBY. That's nice.

KYLE. Yes, it is. How are you?

ABBY. I'm fine, thank you.

KYLE. Who are you?

ABBY. Abigail Esther.

KYLE. That's a pretty name.

ABBY. Abigail Esther Mary Katherine.

KYLE. Even prettier.

ABBY. Abigail Esther Mary Katherine Eglantine Monroe.

KYLE. I'm Kyle.

ABBY. Pleased to meet you, Kyle.

KYLE. And you, Abigail Esther Mary Katherine E…Ek…
   Hek…

ABBY. Please call me Abby.

KYLE. Abby.

ABBY. Sunny again today. The weather's been *blah, blah, blah. (She spits.)* That's enough of that. *(She opens ring box, looks at ring. Wistfully.)* Round and round the ring; round and round, and then it broke. *(She is terribly sad again.) I am sorry. What can I do?*

KYLE. Is that your wedding ring?

ABBY. Round and round I've gone, but I can't find you. Waiting by the path, you don't come. You make me ache. You make me cry. You make me talk into deep holes.

KYLE. Who is he, Abby? Who doesn't come?

ABBY. Soldier Boy. Can't find his way home, the dumbass. I have to bury this so Soldier Boy can find the path to me. Round and round he goes but he never comes out.

KYLE. Do you have to bury the ring because he's in the ground?

ABBY. When he was bleeding, I wasn't there. He called me, but I couldn't hear him.

KYLE. Is that how he can find his way back to you? Is he in the ground, Abby?

ABBY. The earth will make a path to me. *(To ring.)* You're the one. You're the one, baby. I love your hands. I'm all…waiting…for your hands. *(She moves to KYLE, slowly puts her head on his chest. He holds on to her.)* This…is a picture…I saw…in your brain. Your hands…Kyle…on me.

BLACKOUT

SHAKESPEARE IN HOLLYWOOD
By Claudia Haas .

CHARACTERS

HOLLYWOOD AGENT
WILLIAM SHAKESPEARE

TIME: The present.
PLACE: A cluttered Hollywood agent's office.

AT RISE: *A Hollywood AGENT is shuffling papers madly. There could be a cacophony of communication sounds. Phones ringing, faxes beeping, computers squeaking.*

AGENT. Okay, unplug computer! Done! Dismantle the fax; check. Shut off cell phone? Right. Turn off ringer to phone—what else? Nothing. Silence. Yes, silence. Now, maybe I can get some work done. *(Suddenly the lights flicker and go out; a voice booms in the nothingness)*
VOICE (WILL). "Boil, boil, toil and trouble...*Fire Burn!*"

(There is a sound of thunder or a crash box—something jarring and the lights come up again as we find WILL standing in the doorway. He is dressed in Elizabethan clothing.)

WILLIAM *(almost sheepishly)*. ...and cauldron bubble? Oh! A thousand pardons. I know not where I am.

AGENT. I have to give you credit. You know how to make an entrance. *(The AGENT approaches him.)* Is there no relief? Can I get no solitude? Quiet. I crave quiet. The constant ringing, beeping, buzzing, clanging, chiming, tolling, reverberating circle of communication; "You've got mail! You've got mail!" Instant communication is driving me insane! What do you want?

WILLIAM. I am at a loss. I seem to have appeared here. For what reason, I cannot say. Words escape me.

AGENT. O-kay. Let's try another approach. Who are you, what can I do for you? Do you have an appointment and can I make some money off of you?

WILLIAM. Why, I'm William. Shakespeare. I'll just take my leave. I didn't mean—

AGENT. Wait. I've heard of you. Shakespeare, Billy. You write for theatre. In fact, I've seen some of your stuff. Not bad. A little wordy. I was thinking of making one of those plays into a movie.

WILLIAM. Movie?

AGENT. Yeah—the one with the depressed guy—some prince—wears black and talks to himself all the time— which was that?

WILLIAM. In faith, that would be Hamlet.

AGENT. You know, I really need to get some work done, but as long as you dropped in, can we talk?

WILLIAM. I thought we were talking.

AGENT. No, I mean really talk. Numbers, budget, casting, location or computer graphics? Oscars. That sort of thing.

WILLIAM. I understand you...not.

AGENT. Actually, I don't get you either. But this is Tinseltown, so I have learned...have no expectations.

Let's talk turkey, now. I'll tell you what I need and then you can tell me what you can do for me.

WILLIAM. How doth a turkey talk?

AGENT. So, tell me your plan. Reveal your hidden agenda.

WILLIAM. Agenda?

AGENT. Come on, nobody devises an entrance as you did without an agenda. The outfit's cute. Your manner—different. I know! You want me to remember you. Mission accomplished.

WILLIAM. In truth, fair gentle-person, I know not how I came here. I recall sitting in my lodgings and having a wee bit of trouble with the witch's spell..."boil, boil, toil and trouble," and suddenly found myself in this foreign land.

AGENT. What?

WILLIAM. I fear my wits begin to turn. That I be mad would be a pity...aye, 'tis true, a pity. As I wrote in *Hamlet,* "What a noble mind is here o'erthrown."

AGENT. So, we're right back at *Hamlet.* That's what you came to see me about. But I warn you, we'd need a new take. I like the idea—but it's been done—I think in the '70s. You really go back a ways. Got to give you credit. Longevity is rare in this business.

WILLIAM. They say an old man is twice a child.

AGENT. Yeah! O-kay, fine! Anyway, back to *Hamlet.* You know, it needs work, Billy.

WILLIAM. William. My name is William.

AGENT. Yeah, sure, Willie. I mean, I like the script. Lots of action, dead bodies, a cute heroine. Sword fights. Not too bad. Of course, there's one problem...

WILLIAM. I beg your pardon?

AGENT. Words. There's—you know—a lot of them. Film
is a visual medium. A soulful glance, the right under-
scoring of music—you get the picture. We need to get
rid of most of the words.

WILLIAM. But—I write. That is what I do. I know not
how to write without words.

AGENT. That's where I come in. I do Development. We
will develop this together. The bones of the script are
pretty good. And then when Hamlet goes mad—well,
that's pretty powerful stuff.

WILLIAM. Hamlet doesn't go mad. Ophelia goes mad.

AGENT. What? Who? You mean the sweet young thing
who bursts into song in the middle of the play? No,
no—she doesn't go mad. I see her singing her "Nonny"
—maybe Aretha Franklin-like—you know—powerful
affirmation of women—

*(At this point the AGENT rips into an Aretha-style ver-
sion of how Ophelia's song might go—or could be gos-
pel.)*

"Hey, nonny nonny!
I said *hey* nonny, nonny!
He is gone, he is gone
And we cast away moan:
God ha' mercy on his soul!
Hey, nonny nonny!"

Something like that. After that scene, Ophelia emerges
as a strong, modern woman and Hamlet cracks. You
don't realize that because you stuck in all those words.
They're confusing.

WILLIAM. There must be gall in mine ink for you to interpret so.

AGENT *(begins to chuckle)*. Gall in the ink! You're funny. I think. Maybe. You know, I'm never quite sure what your words mean. *That's* what we need to take care of.

WILLIAM. I am not yet so old that I cannot learn new ways.

AGENT. Great attitude! I love it! We can be a team, Willie. With your ideas and my vision, I see Oscar written all over it.

WILLIAM. Oscar? There is no Oscar in my works. Wherefore art Oscar?

AGENT. Think future, Willie! Box-office percentages, *Hamlet II, Hamlet Returns, The Return of the Prince!* TV spinoffs. After you get Oscar, the deals will roll in.

WILLIAM. My thoughts are whirled like a potter's wheel; I know not where I am, nor what I do.

AGENT. Right. I know not anything also. I mean, I don't know what I mean. But that's okay. Part of being an agent, you know? You put things together and wham! On to the next thing. You never have to delve. Never really have to bring anything to fruition. It's great.

WILLIAM. By your troth?

AGENT. By my troth? Well, *no! No!* There! I've said it aloud. I've had it with the electronic age. Instant questions, instant answers! Answer your 100 e-mails, take a meeting, return phone calls, "do" lunch, scan scripts, throw a pitch, pitch a plan! Can a plan and re-plan! Sow your seeds, plant a bush! Crown a king and king a checker!

WILLIAM. What meanst thou?

AGENT. I meanst—I have had it! I *meanst* I'm done! Done! Done as a doornail! Remember when "they" said the computer would make life easier? Remember when "they" said the cell phone would save time? Remember those days?

WILLIAM. I cannot remember such things were.

AGENT. Were and *are!* It's the reality of our world.

WILLIAM. I hold the world but as a world... A stage, where every man must play his part and mine a sad one, for I am far from home.

AGENT. Let me give you some advice, go home! Leave. Vamoose before this town turns you into a piece of tinsel. Run! And never look back!

WILLIAM. But I know not how to do as thou asks.

AGENT. Just backtrack. I do it all the time.

WILLIAM. I was writing...

AGENT. So—write!

WILLIAM. It was the witch's spell... ...Boil, boil, toil and trouble...

AGENT. What are you doing?

WILLIAM. Casting an enchantment. It seems to make me movable.

AGENT. Use your legs, man! That's how you retrace your steps!

WILLIAM. You would better advise me to "taste my legs" for it is not with my legs that I came. I shall turn my back. There is a world elsewhere. *(WILLIAM turns around.)*

AGENT. All right. I'll bite. Your world, where is it?

WILLIAM. Where'er I wander, boast of this I can:
Though banished yet a true-born Englishman.

AGENT. Whoa! Flashback...eighth grade...Englishman... English class...Shakespeare...I studied...a play...something about a dream...a summer dream...fairies...and a lot of stuff I didn't get...

WILLIAM. *A Midsummer Night's Dream.*

AGENT. Yeah. Maybe. But that was written—you know before we were born.

WILLIAM. Indeed, I was born first and then wrote it.

AGENT. But that would make you—old. Nobody old works in this town.

WILLIAM. In truth, I work in London.

AGENT. Just like the guy I studied—but he's you know —dead.

WILLIAM. Why, I live and grow ripe.

AGENT. And your words…they're mangled just like this other Shakespeare guy. Say, are you a Shakespeare impersonator?

WILLIAM. I am just a player on this great stage. No more. No less. But I yearn for home. When I was at home, I was in a better place.

AGENT. Wherefore?

WILLIAM. Britain's a world by itself. The island of England breeds very valiant creatures. It is a blessed plot of land, this earth, this realm, this England.

AGENT. You know…I've always wanted to go to England. Sometime…in someone's time.

WILLIAM. Join me then. I'll put a girdle around the earth in forty minutes.

AGENT. Go? We can just go? Leaving behind my faxes, my deal-makings, my pitches, my five phones, my palm pilot? Can I do this! Can I kiss this goodbye? Yes! A thousand times yes! Listen, Billy-boy, I don't know where I'm off to—but it has to be better than this! Is it quiet, your England?

WILLIAM. The days bring noise and the nights sound silent.

AGENT. I like the sound of that—silent.

WILLIAM. For silence is the herald of joy.

AGENT. Silence—the herald of joy—I like that. Yes. Let's try your England, Billy-boy. Show me the way!

WILLIAM. Your heart's desires be with you! The world's an oyster which I with pen will open.

(The AGENT joins WILL.)

Boil, boil, toil and trouble,
Fire burn and cauldron bubble.

(There is a flashing of light and then darkness.)

AGENT. You know, Billy. I think this is the beginning of a beautiful friendship.

BLACKOUT

BOXED IN
By Rachel Feldbin Urist

CHARACTERS

BINKY: In her teens.
LIZ: In her teens.

TIME: The present.
PLACE: A general space used by acting students. There is a bench or, perhaps, a large cardboard box. The girls are improvising dramatic possibilities.

AT RISE: *LIZ and BINKY sit on the floor opposite each other in stony silence.*

BINKY. It's a chest. *(Pause.)*
LIZ. It's a bench. *(Pause.)* Anybody looking can *see* it's a bench. I mean, look at it. It looks like a bench. It feels like a bench. It's a bench.
BINKY. You can't do anything with a bench.
LIZ. What do you mean?
BINKY. Sit and talk. That's all you can do. That's boring.
LIZ. What's so great about a chest?
BINKY. It simply *is.* You can wonder what's in it. Or it can be locked, and we'd have to figure out how to open it. We could steal it. Or we could find it. It could have a dead body in it. Or treasures. Or papers that look like garbage but turn out to hold a fortune. Or we could just sit on it. Sit and talk. *(Pause.)*

LIZ. You're the one who always wants to talk.

BINKY. Don't start.

LIZ. Start what? I just said you always—

BINKY. I know what you said. Stop it.

LIZ. Okay.

BINKY. You should have told me.

LIZ. I thought you didn't want to get into it.

BINKY. I don't. *(Silence.)*

LIZ. We could always wonder about all the people who slept on the bench.

BINKY. How many people puked on it.

LIZ. You really love the bench idea. I can feel it.

BINKY. Yeah. Clever of you to notice, Liz.

LIZ. Why don't we just try it?

BINKY. Why?

LIZ. Why not? If it doesn't work we'll know it doesn't work.

BINKY. Okay. We'll try it. *(Pause.)*

LIZ. So it's a bench. *(Pause.)* Who are we?

BINKY. You be the pretty young thing sitting on the bench, and I'll be your beau.

LIZ. Binky,

BINKY *(as the beau)*. Well, hello, sugar.

LIZ. Oh, God.

BINKY. Hey, I've missed you real bad. I've been dreamin' about you.

(BINKY strokes LIZ's hair, caresses her. When BINKY gets too forward, LIZ pushes her away.)

LIZ. I don't really want you as a beau. *(Silence.)*

BINKY. Okay. Who are we, then?

LIZ. Twins. Lacy and Tracy. We're waiting for our dates. Who are also twins.

BINKY *(gestures disgust—code for vomit. Pause)*. Okay. *(She sits on the bench/box and begins the improvisation in a little-girl voice, almost Betty Boop.)* Gee, Tracy, I don't know what can be taking them so long. Do you think we'll be stood up?

LIZ. If you're just going to make fun of it, there's no point.

BINKY *(in the same silly voice)*. Making fun! Tracy, I wouldn't make fun of a date with *(taking a deep breath)* Louie and Stuie Brandon! Whatever can you think of me?

LIZ. Forget it.

BINKY *(grabbing LIZ by the arm and persisting with the improvisation)*. Now, Tracy, you can't walk off when there's adventure lying just ahead. You wouldn't leave your innocent sister to fend for herself, all alone on this night with two Brandon boys! Now, would you?

LIZ. This is insulting. You realize that.

BINKY. Aw, Tracy. Just think. Cotton candy, the merry-go-round, maybe a Ferris wheel! *(Sighs exaggeratedly.)* How romantic!

LIZ. Stop it already!

BINKY. Why're you always being so nasty, Tracy? Here we are all ready for our big date and you've got to go pick a fight. What a party pooper. You know what I'm gonna tell the boys when they get here? You want to know? I'm gonna tell them that you got scared. No. No, I'm gonna tell them that you cried because you thought they only asked you out out of pity. That's what I'll say if you go away. *(As herself.)* Though I noticed you weren't very shy with Freddy.

LIZ. Well…

BINKY. Do you want to tell me about Freddy?

LIZ. No! *(Beat.)* Why are we waiting here, sitting on a bench if this is a date? Shouldn't they be picking us up at home?

BINKY *(as herself)*. We're here because this is a bench. And we're sitting on it. That's what you wanted to do, wasn't it? And wait for the Brandon boys. *(As Tracy.)* Louie and Stuie, isn't it? Gee, I hope I remember which one's which when they get here.

LIZ. Okay, it's a chest.

BINKY *(looks down at her bosom)*. Gee, thanks, Tracy.

LIZ. It's a chest! *(Pushing BINKY under/into the bench/ box.)* It's a stupid chest, and you're getting in it.

BINKY. Whoa, girl. Whoa. Hey! Cut it out! I am not getting in any stupid chest.

LIZ. Too late. You are. *(She sits on the bench/box.)*

BINKY. Get off!

LIZ *(in a Southern accent—a Blanche DuBois imitation)*. Now what could that be, I wonder. Sounds like a maiden in distress. *(Talking to an invisible man.)* Oh, Captain, I can't bear to think what might have happened to my dear, sweet cousin. She was so gentle, and sweet. And she couldn't swim. *(Sigh.)* Poor Colette. A victim of whim. The fates are cruel, aren't they?

BINKY. Let me out!

LIZ. Captain, did you hear something? It sounds just like my poor cousin. It must be the power of grief. It plays tricks on the mind, doesn't it. *(BINKY pounds on the bench/box from inside, and continues protesting as LIZ talks.)* It seems to me that Colette is very close. That if I just turned around I would see her with my own eyes. But I know that can never be. Those are shark-infested waters. Oh, why was I left behind!

BINKY. Your dialogue stinks and so does this box! *(Shrilly.)* Now get off and let me up!

LIZ. She had such a lyrical voice, Colette did. Soft and delicate, like a Grecian lyre. I remember when we were girls, we'd play on the grass, and Colette would sing, and all the little birds would just—

(BINKY bursts out of the bench/box, sending LIZ flying.)

BINKY *(angry)*. Just because I mentioned Freddy, right? Look, you made your bed, now lie in it.

LIZ. I thought you were my friend.

BINKY. I am!

LIZ. It was all over between you anyway.

BINKY. How do you know?

LIZ. Because you told me.

BINKY. Ah.

LIZ. Look, I'm sorry. All right? I am sorry. But it's over. So let sleeping dogs lie.

BINKY. Sleeping dogs eventually wake up. Never mind. Let's forget it. We'll start again. Your dialogue does stink, though.

LIZ. I shouldn't have to think up dialogue. As long as I can play it.

BINKY. Any actor worth her salt ought to be able to improvise a little credible dialogue.

LIZ. Why are you talking to me like this?

BINKY. You just shoved me in a box and sat on me!

LIZ. I didn't sit on you. I was sitting on the *chest*.

BINKY. Yeah.

LIZ. Are you going to do this with me or not?

BINKY. Of course I will, sweetie.

LIZ. Good.

BINKY. I'm just spicing it up.

LIZ. Don't. And drop the Freddy stuff, okay?

BINKY. Right.

LIZ. Let's start from scratch. No chest. No bench.

BINKY. What is it, then?

LIZ. You think of something.

BINKY. Okay. It's a cage. And you've just escaped from it. *(Pause.)*

LIZ. What am I?

BINKY. A panther.

LIZ. A panther. And what am I supposed to do?

BINKY. You fall into a ditch and break your leg. I will find you.

(LIZ groans. Pause. LIZ crouches and prowls on all fours, simulating, as best she can, a hunted, four-legged animal. BINKY stalks her.)

BINKY *(calling)*. Oh, Jasmine!

LIZ *(exasperated at being called "Jasmine")*. What am I, your pet panther? If you come any closer I'll pounce on you.

BINKY. You can't pounce on me. Your leg'll be broken. *(They continue as before.)*

LIZ. Aaaaah!

(She falls into a "ditch" and, holding one leg, cries out in pain. BINKY cocks an ear to the sound and then lunges at LIZ, throwing herself full on the injured panther.)

LIZ. Ow! Stop it! Get off! This is stupid! I don't want to be a panther.

BINKY *(pinning LIZ)*. Then be my friend.

LIZ. Too late.

BINKY. Liz, I apologize. It was dumb. I was stupid.

LIZ. Yes, you were.

BINKY. Do you forgive me?

LIZ. Will you *let me up?!*

BINKY. Say you're my friend.

LIZ *(contemplates the matter for a moment. Softly)*. Okay. I accept your apology.

BINKY. And all's forgiven?

LIZ *(after a moment's hesitation, a smile)*. Yeah. We're still buddies.

(Their tussle is now a hug.)

BINKY. They're waiting. I really am sorry.

LIZ. Yeah. Come on. Let's knock 'em dead.

(They do a thumbs-up, then an intricate, private dance or a handshake. They link arms.)

BLACKOUT

THE PIER GROUP
By Elizabeth Hemmerdinger

The Pier Group premiered in 2004 at the Pulse Ensemble Fun Festival in New York City. It was directed by Alexa Kelly and featured Beatriz Abella, Meghan Love and Cameron Peterson.

CHARACTERS

AMANDA: Smug, authoritarian and defiant enough to be coated with baby oil. Her assignment: Buddy Board (a clipboard), the list of swimmer pairs.

KIKI: Lethargic, laconic and sarcastic. Assigned to Pole Duty, she holds an eight-foot pole meant to be put in the water for a tired swimmer to grab. She also has a clipboard that lists all swimmers.

SARAH: Sincere and nervous, wears a large hat, dark glasses, a long-sleeved shirt and zinc oxide to protect her nose and cheeks.

TIME: The present.

PLACE: A small, unstable floating raft in deep water at Camp Baldwin.

AT RISE: *AMANDA, KIKI and SARAH oversee Free Swim, with campers all around them. They're hot, bored and underqualified to be counselors.*

SARAH. Hey, lookit that kid go!

AMANDA. Yeah.

KIKI. Lookit her go. Whadya suppose she's doing way out there beyond the swim area?

AMANDA. For a "metabolically challenged" kid, she sure can swim.

KIKI. Fat? How fat?

SARAH. That is so rude!

AMANDA. Pretty fat. And it isn't rude, it's what they told us to say.

KIKI. Fatter'n Porky?

SARAH. What if they hear you?

AMANDA. What if, Tool?

KIKI. Anybody around here listen to you?

SARAH. Hard-ly! But, hey, what if it's Becky?

KIKI. Who's this Becky, anyway?

SARAH. The one who keeps crying all the time. I think she wants to go home.

AMANDA. Becky Who?

SARAH. You know. Becky What's-Her-Face.

KIKI *(checks her clipboard list)*. She's not down for waterfront.

AMANDA *(lazily checks the Buddy Board)*. That checks. She's not on the Buddy Board.

SARAH. Boy, does that ever look like her.

KIKI. It can't be, because she's not on the Buddy Board.

AMANDA. That checks. She's not down for waterfront.

SARAH. Okay, okay! *(They return to their thoughts.)* Isn't Becky in your cabin?

KIKI. We got a fat kid, call her Porky.

SARAH. Hey!

KIKI. Well, excuse me…she deserves it. Eats everybody's seconds.

SARAH. Maybe we oughta do something. I mean, maybe she's drowning.

KIKI. You wouldn't kid anybody, wouldja?

(KIKI and AMANDA laugh. KIKI and SARAH look at AMANDA.)

AMANDA. I can't do anything.

KIKI. How come?

AMANDA. You want to look on the Buddy Board? Right there on top it says you can't leave the Buddy Board. You gotta "hold the Buddy Board at all times." Okay?

KIKI. Follow those rules straight across a burning bridge, I bet.

AMANDA. I have responsibilities, Crackhead. Hey, how come you don't go?

KIKI. "Raft Duty stays on the raft." Strict orders. You are not the only one who knows how to keep a stupid job. *(KIKI notices a camper and brandishes her pole.)* You, down there. Where's your buddy? Stay close, you hear? I get upset or something, I could drop this on somebody's head…again.

SARAH. Hey, listen. This could be serious. And I don't want to be responsible in case something happens. Somebody better go.

KIKI. That would be…you?

SARAH. Who?

KIKI. You. That's who. Boy…she sure can swim.

SARAH. Yeah…and I can barely float. Do you think I belong on this float way out in the water? No. But try to tell that to Norm! All the time he was rowing me out here, I tried to say. But would he listen? I mean, God! If I drown my mother will sue this place, I swear it. A person who can barely float, trying to catch up with… with…whoever it is swimming like she's being chased by a shark or a snapping turtle or whatever it is down in that water which you can never see the bottom of. So you never know anything.

AMANDA. You know. It's Becky What's-Her-Face.

SARAH. How do you know?

AMANDA. You told me. That's how I know.

SARAH. When?

AMANDA. Just now, loser. *(To KIKI.)* Right?

KIKI. You tell me, "loser."

SARAH *(miserable)*. Who, me?

AMANDA. What?

SARAH. Who, that's what.

KIKI. Becky, that's who. Anyway, it isn't Porky. Never did get her mattress back up on the top bunk. The kids, they threw it down, and all her clothes, when she got up one night to pee. Slept on the floor 'til Norm made me clean up. Just a loser, not like that kid!

SARAH. Lookit her go. *(SARAH gets splashed by swimmers near the float.)* Quit it! Even if I could swim, I could never catch her. She's halfway across the lake!

AMANDA. You could try.

SARAH. Oh, no I couldn't, either. I gotta stay right here on the float. Norm said.

AMANDA. Like we didn't already know… "There's no leaving your post!" Where the hell is Rita?

SARAH. Yu-huh! Without the Lady of the Lake, we've got to be extra careful. *(Reacts ferociously to a splash.)* Watch it!

AMANDA. And exactly how smart was that? Taking all the waterfront counselors to a damned swim meet, while we get left behind—watching these losers. Which makes us what? Shower heads? And they're probably gonna get McDonald's on the way back. We oughta just walk!

SARAH. Quit! In the middle of the summer?

AMANDA. Like they'd care.

KIKI. Like we'd get work.

SARAH. Quit that splashing, Monica! Or else.

AMANDA. Like we'd get unemployment.

SARAH. That kid better be careful. No kidding! She may get tired and drown.

KIKI. No kidding, Sherlock! Those are awful short arms. Anybody else take Senior Lifesaving?

AMANDA. Not me…

SARAH. I went to the Career Planning office for a dot com company. For graphics. All I got was this. Stupid Nasdaq. Eighty dollars a week, bugs, mildew, and now I'm way out here instead of being in the Arts and Crafts shed.

KIKI. Like you've got the solo franchise on babysitting in the woods!

AMANDA. Yeah, like "Survivor," without the money. Or the sex. You even know what sex is?

SARAH. Would I ever tease you?

AMANDA. Fat chance.

KIKI. Fatter than Becky? *(KIKI laughs alone.)*

SARAH. What's so funny?

KIKI. I dunno. It's funny, is all.

AMANDA. What's so funny about a fat kid drowning?

KIKI. The kid who's been getting the Silent Treatment since Day One? Twenty-three days and no one's said boo to her? She's that tough, and she's drowning? I don't think so!

AMANDA. I never said that!

SARAH. Then what did you say?

AMANDA. I said, "What's so funny?"

SARAH. I dunno? I'm way out here on this stupid float when all I want is to be in the shed. In the shade. Or in Silicon Alley. In an office. Yeah. How should I know what's so funny? Nothing's funny out here.

(AMANDA blows her whistle.)

KIKI. Hey, whadja do that for?

AMANDA. I felt like it.

KIKI. You can't just blow a whistle like that! *(To the swimmers.)* Keep moving down there. False alarm! I'll tell you when Free Swim is over. *(To AMANDA and SARAH.)* If Norm has to come running down here, before the activity time is up, he's gonna tell Rita, and then we've had it! *(Carefully.)* When you blow that whistle, it means something: it means there's trouble.

SARAH. Trouble! What kind of trouble?

KIKI. I dunno. *(Indicates AMANDA.)* Ask her.

SARAH *(exactly the same delivery)*. Trouble! What kind of trouble?

AMANDA. You always do everything she tells you to?

SARAH. Nope! Only when there's trouble.

AMANDA. That's so stupid.

KIKI. You sure are smart.

SARAH. This trouble's our responsibility. What are we going to do? Where is she, anyway?

AMANDA. Yeah. What are we going to do?

KIKI. Don't ask me. You blew the whistle.

AMANDA. Prove it.

KIKI. You can't kid me. There's trouble. That's when you blow a whistle.

AMANDA. 'Course I know there's trouble. I'm the one who blew the whistle.

KIKI. So, smarty. What are you gonna do now?

AMANDA. I'm gonna give you a turn.

(KIKI thinks. Then she blows her whistle.)

SARAH. Hey, what's the trouble?

KIKI. I dunno. Somebody could be drowning. *(Announcing.)* Buddy Check.

SARAH. You better save her.

AMANDA. Who, me?

SARAH *(to KIKI)*. You're the one with Senior Lifesaving.

KIKI *(counts buddies)*. 1-2-3... How come it's always got to be her way?

AMANDA. It isn't always my way.

SARAH. I never get my way. I'm stuck out here on this stupid float.

KIKI. You blew the whistle first. *(To a swimmer.)* Lilly, where's your buddy? Lose her again, and you've got Toilets for the rest of the summer.

AMANDA. So what if I blew the whistle first. It doesn't prove squat.

KIKI. I can't see those arms! Higher...four, five, six...

SARAH. Fight, fight, fight. Just like a bunch of little kids. Isn't anybody going after Becky? I hate my mother. We're gonna be in an awful lot of trouble if...if...

AMANDA. "We"? You're the one who started this.

KIKI. Okay, Buddy Check's complete. *(She blows two short whistle blasts.)*

SARAH. Wait! I got it! She's swimming home.

KIKI *(waves the swimmers back to swimming)*. Wait a wet minute here. Why don't I ever get to choose?

AMANDA. Okay! Enough already. Let's just call it.

KIKI. Call it what?

AMANDA. I don't care. What do you want to call it? Let's call it "Ted." Hey, you out there! How does Ted sound to you?

SARAH. Ted? It's Becky Ted! That's her name. She made a tray with her initials last week. Come on, Amanda. Look for "Ted" on the board.

KIKI. Becky Ted sits on the porch all day reading and crying. That kid is a swimmer. That kid is ready for the Olympics.

SARAH *(shouting to Becky)*. Come back, Becky. We can talk. We can press moths. A person can get very absorbed in that. Time passes…it's only five more weeks.

AMANDA. She's not on the list.

KIKI. Anyway, I don't see her, anymore.

AMANDA. We can't lose a kid who's not on the list. Get it? Get it!

SARAH. But we saw her.

AMANDA. Not me.

SARAH *(jumps up, rocking the float violently)*. We did see her!

AMANDA. All that jumping is gonna tip that float. And then you'll be the one drowning. And personally, I saw nobody. Period.

SARAH. I don't see her, either! *(Shouting.)* Becky!

KIKI. That's because nobody's out there.

AMANDA. Will you two keep it down!

SARAH *(whispering loudly)*. Hold on, Becky.

AMANDA. People—anxious people in the wrong job— see things. When the sun's too strong.

SARAH. We have been watching a child drown!

AMANDA. There is nothing out there.

SARAH. "Nothing"! There's trees. And us. And kids in the water here and… What in the world do you call this…big, murky…water thing…lake thing…body of water thing…with "nobody"…with a dead girl in it? Get a boat! Where's Norm with that boat?

AMANDA. What exactly are you going to do in jail? Press cockroaches? Because they're sure as hell not going to give you swimming lessons.

SARAH. Jail?

AMANDA. It was a mirage.

KIKI. Becky Ted is not down for waterfront.

SARAH. Gosh.

KIKI. There was nobody to see.

SARAH. Nobody.

AMANDA. Here comes the boat. *(AMANDA blows her whistle.)* Let's see those buddy hands waving up in the air so Norm can see.

(A BUGLE sounds the end of the activity.)

SARAH. There! That's Becky! Climbing up the dock at Larson's Landing.

KIKI. Like you could really see five miles away!

SARAH. There she is, there she is! Can't you see?

AMANDA. I'm counting buddies.

SARAH *(calling to Becky)*. Run!

KIKI. Quit making stuff up.

SARAH. I'm not!

AMANDA *(announcing)*. All buddies accounted for. Free Swim is over.

SARAH. Save yourself! Run!

KIKI. Hey, you guys!

AMANDA. Everybody out of the water and dress for dinner.

KIKI. Quit that whining, Monica. Nobody cares.

SARAH. Safe home, Becky!

AMANDA & KIKI. Sarah!

BLACKOUT

SLEEPOVERS AND SERIAL KILLERS
By Tammy Ryan

CHARACTERS

JOAN: 30. Mother of Emily. Recently moved to the "country" to escape the dangers of the city and to start a career as a writer. Overprotective at times, she has been close to her daughter until recently.

EMILY: 12. Going on 30. She is smart, impetuous, used to getting her own way. She is angry at her mom for the move, but what she wants more than anything is to make friends at her new school.

TIME: The present.
PLACE: A living room.

AT RISE: *JOAN is knitting, a candle is burning nearby. EMILY enters, smiling brightly.*

JOAN. Here she is.

EMILY. Hi Mom. *(Kisses JOAN, who holds onto her a little longer.)* How was your day?

JOAN *(smiling)*. My day was okay…what's going on, Emily?

EMILY. What? I had a good day, just askin' how yours was. I'm not always thinking of myself, you know.

JOAN. My day was fine. I didn't learn how to knit.

EMILY. Mom, when are you going to judge yourself not by what you can do, but who you *are*.

JOAN. You want a smack? I mean snack?

EMILY. Sure.

JOAN. Oh, now I'm really suspicious.

EMILY. What, I'm hungry.

JOAN. What are you doing?

EMILY *(taking stuff out of a box)*. I'm helping you.

JOAN. Okay, what happened, what do you want, I know you want something. I can smell it.

EMILY. If you say yes, I'll help you unpack all the rest of the boxes and I won't quit until it's done. I got invited to go to a sleepover at this girl Marilyn's. There's about five other girls going and they invited me!

JOAN. When?

EMILY. Next Friday—it's *not* a Halloween party, just a sleepover.

JOAN. And where is it?

EMILY. Marilyn's dad's…cabin.

JOAN. What do you mean, cabin?

EMILY. Her dad has a cabin. Not far.

JOAN. In the woods? What, are they divorced? Her "dad's cabin."

EMILY. What does that matter?

JOAN. Will one of her parents be there?

EMILY. Her older sister will be there.

JOAN. How much older.

EMILY. She's sixteen. But, she's gonna be seventeen!

JOAN. And where is it, in the woods? Does it have electricity? A phone?

EMILY. I don't know; it's on her parents' land up past the school! And, yes, it's in the woods, everything's in the woods around here.

JOAN. I don't think so.

EMILY. I can bring your cell phone!

JOAN. No.

EMILY. You want me to make friends and then when I finally do, you tell me I can't go!

JOAN. I'm not telling you you can't make friends, I'm telling you I don't want you in the middle of the woods at night without adult supervision—

EMILY. But her sister's gonna be there!

JOAN. —with a serial killer on the loose!

EMILY. Ugh. I knew it. It's *not* a serial killer. They were totally unrelated murders.

JOAN. Two weeks ago you told me it was a serial killer.

EMILY. Well, now they've decided it isn't.

JOAN. Two girls have still been killed.

EMILY. If you stopped your life every time some girl got murdered.

JOAN. Maybe you should.

EMILY. Your life would be at a standstill! Somebody is always out there murdering people. This is not about dead girls, this is about *you* being afraid.

JOAN. Of a serial killer in my neighborhood, yes, I admit I'm afraid.

EMILY. You're afraid of everything. First you're afraid of the city, now you're afraid of the country—

JOAN. I'm not having this conversation. Go to your room and start your homework.

EMILY. You're also afraid of the harmful effects of television, of hormones in the milk and genetically altered potatoes. You can't put something in your mouth without washing it a hundred times because you're afraid of pesticides, but you're also afraid of the water: city water, well water, ground water. Doesn't matter, you're afraid of it.

JOAN. That's enough.

EMILY. No, because you're also afraid of me making friends, because then I won't need you anymore, because what you're really afraid of is me growing up. You're afraid then you'll have to deal with *your own life!* This is your fear, Mom, and it's strangling me!

JOAN *(overlapping on "fear")*. You are not grown up, you are twelve years old and I think you better take a timeout before you say another word.

EMILY. Fine. But I know why we moved up here! So you can keep me in *prison! (She storms off.)*

JOAN. This is not the way to get what you want, Emily.

EMILY *(offstage)*. And don't bother making me dinner! I'll just eat *bread and water!*

JOAN. I can't worry about you liking me, I have to protect you.

(Pause. Silence. JOAN throws down her knitting. Quietly EMILY returns, trying to control her emotions.)

EMILY. Mom?

JOAN. Yeah.

EMILY. I'm sorry.

JOAN. Me too. For yelling. I hate yelling.

EMILY. It's just the first time I've been invited anywhere and I really want to go. I want some friends, Mom.

JOAN. I know you do, Emily. You'll make friends. Before you ask me again, I want you to listen: I don't have a relationship with my mother. I was into all kinds of trouble and I basically did not have a mother watching out for me. She was busy with the littler ones when I was a teenager, and dealing with my father, who drank, and so she was never there for me. I went behind her back. I lied to her. I was into all kinds of trouble, and she had no idea what was going on in my life. And as much as I told myself I didn't care, as much as I thought I didn't need a mother, I actually needed her very much.

EMILY. Mom, I know I need you.

JOAN. I don't want you to feel about me, the way I felt about my mother. That I couldn't trust her with the truth of my life.

EMILY. I'm not lying. Marilyn's sister is gonna be there.

JOAN. I'm not worried about Marilyn's sister.

EMILY. Then what are you worried about?

JOAN. You think I'm afraid of everything. When you're a parent you'll understand this more. It's dangerous out there. I hate having to tell you that, because I don't want to make you afraid, but I need to make you safe.

EMILY. That's what they do out in the country though, they're not afraid of the woods out here. And all the other kids are my age. Their parents trust them.

JOAN. I don't think you're going to do anything bad. I'm afraid of something bad happening to you.

EMILY. I bet Dad says yes.

JOAN. Don't do that. Don't pit us against each other.

EMILY. But what am I supposed to do? This is important to me!

JOAN. There'll be other parties.

EMILY. Now you sound like your mother.

JOAN. And I'm not happy about it, but I don't know what else to say, except in my gut, I cannot let you go out into the woods right now. Do you want me to do that— go against my instincts? *(EMILY suddenly thrusts her hand over the flame. JOAN pulls her hand away.)* What are you doing? Emily, you're gonna burn yourself. Emily!

EMILY *(continuing to thrust her hand into the flame)*. Don't stop me! See, you keep stopping me! You can't stop me forever!!

JOAN *(blows out candle)*. I'm not gonna sit here and watch you burn your hand!

EMILY. I'm gonna grow up knowing *nothing* about the world!

JOAN. You have an imagination. You don't have to experience the world to know it's dangerous!

EMILY. That's just it, I *want* to experience it! I *want to!*

JOAN. I'm not getting into another argument I can't win.

EMILY. All I get to experience is on television, and you hate television.

JOAN. For now you can read books.

EMILY. You're always telling me "Life is not a fairy tale!"

JOAN. That's right, it's not.

EMILY. But the way you're bringing me up, I'm gonna be a scared little rabbit! Please, Mom, I wanna go.

JOAN. No. I have to say no. Two girls your age have disappeared not far from here and have been found dead in the woods. Now that is a real danger—and until they find the maniac responsible, I have to protect you the only way I know how—you are not going to a sleepover in a cabin in the woods without parental supervision; do not ask me again.

EMILY. You can't really protect me. You just think you can. Anything can happen. You're not watching over me every single minute. All your worrying and trying to protect me, is good for nothing, because I could still wind up—

JOAN. Don't say another word!

(EMILY pulls away from JOAN.)

BLACKOUT

HARLEY'S ART FARCE
By Mark Plaiss

CHARACTERS

HARLEY: A teenager.
JASON: A teenager.

TIME: The present.
PLACE: Anywhere.

AT RISE: *HARLEY and JASON are building a house of cards.*

HARLEY. Guess what I had a ticket to.

JASON. No idea.

HARLEY *(throughout skit he pronounces it MON-et, rhyming with "bonnet")*. The Monet show.

JASON *(pauses, placing another card on the house as he considers what he's just heard)*. You talking 'bout the Monet exhibit at the Art Institute?

HARLEY. Absolutely.

JASON. You had tickets.

HARLEY. *Ticket.* Singular, not plural.

JASON. You had one ticket to the Monet exhibit?

HARLEY. That I did.

JASON. How? I've been trying to get tickets for a week. Amber's into the Impressionists.

HARLEY. Dexter gave me his ticket.

45

JASON. Dexter Philips? He wouldn't know a Monet from Michelangelo.

HARLEY. He's a member. Well, his parents are. Besides, he doesn't go there for the art.

JASON. What, then.

HARLEY. Girls.

JASON. What girls?

HARLEY. He meets at the Art Institute.

JASON. A hook-up joint?

HARLEY. Makes out like a bandit.

JASON. So what are you doin' with Dexter's ticket?

HARLEY. I'm in a rut. Thought I might try Dexter's approach.

JASON. And?

HARLEY. So I'm roaming through the place, right? Jesuses, saints, churches, trees, kings, queens and mountains all over the place. You know, the masters.

JASON. The usual menu.

HARLEY. Exactly. So I wander into the section where the modern guys are. Now up on this wall is this one… thing.

JASON. What thing?

HARLEY. I don't know. It's—

JASON. Is it a painting or what?

HARLEY. That's my point, it—

JASON. Does it hang on the wall?

HARLEY. It does.

JASON. Is it framed?

HARLEY. Yes, but—

JASON. It's a painting.

HARLEY. Wait.

JASON. What?

HARLEY. What I'm trying to tell you. This painting was just black.

JASON. Whataya mean?

HARLEY. I mean the painting is just a canvas painted black.

JASON. Solid black?

HARLEY. That's what I'm saying. No different shades of black. No variations in texture. Just a plain black canvas...

JASON. ...hanging on the wall.

HARLEY. You got it. Now. Is that a picture?

JASON *(stops with a card in his hands, thinking)*. Someone just painted a square canvas a solid shade of black.

HARLEY. Yes.

JASON. No. *(HARLEY and JASON knock fists.)* So?

HARLEY. So I'm standing there staring at this...this—

JASON. Thing...

HARLEY. ...right, and I say out loud, but not real loud, "This is *art?* Somebody thought this worthy to be placed in an art museum?"

JASON. Uh-uh.

HARLEY. Up steps this woman from my left. Says, "Yes, it is art," but not snotty or anything.

JASON. She work there?

HARLEY. Too good-looking to work there.

JASON. And?

HARLEY. I ask her, "What makes this art?" Know what she says?

JASON. It radiates negative ions?

HARLEY. No.

JASON. Emits a sense of other-ness?

HARLEY. No.

JASON. Depicts man's inhumanity to man?

HARLEY. Try, "it provokes a response."

JASON. A response?

HARLEY. I pick my nose in the foyer of the Art Institute, that provokes a response.

JASON. You told her that?

HARLEY. No. But it would.

JASON. You know it.

HARLEY. You better believe I know it.

JASON. But?

HARLEY. But like I said, she was hot so I slacked back.

JASON. The Dexter method.

HARLEY. Right. Now. Know what's next to it?

JASON. The girl?

HARLEY. The painting.

JASON. Another painting?

HARLEY. Solid white.

JASON. Like the black one…

HARLEY. …only white, right.

JASON. Somebody sure forgot to buy some paint that day.

HARLEY. Tell me. So I point to the white and black canvases and say, "What response do these provoke in you?"

JASON. She says?

HARLEY. God.

JASON. Well, she lost me.

HARLEY. Bogus-central. I can see the "artist" now. Paint roller in hand, standing back a bit, admiring his "work" and sayin' to himself: "two to one the morons'll think this is something profound."

JASON. Tell her that?

HARLEY. No. But it's true.

JASON. So true.

HARLEY. Too true. So I say, "How you figure?"

JASON. That it's God and all.

HARLEY. Right. Says, "God is simple, primary and one."

JASON. Uh-uh.

HARLEY. I mean, what's the bogus-o-meter on that one?

JASON. Eleven?

HARLEY. On a scale from one to ten, at least.

JASON. So?

HARLEY. So a little this, a little that, and we tour the world of Mr. Monet together. She oohs and ahhs over these waterlilies and stuff, and I'm thinking Mr. Monet sure had a one-track mind. I mean, he really liked the color green.

JASON. You tell her that?

HARLEY. No. But believe it.

JASON. Better well believe it.

HARLEY. Yes sir.

JASON. What *do* you tell her?

HARLEY. "They exude a soothing calmness."

JASON. As opposed to a grating calmness.

HARLEY. What can I say: she bought it.

JASON. And?

HARLEY. Across the street for some eats.

JASON. She had?

HARLEY. A salad.

JASON. Cheap, too.

HARLEY. The dinner, not her, Jason. Not that it matters much, you understand.

JASON. 'Course. Then?

HARLEY. Well…uh…

JASON. Outstanding. So when do I meet her?

HARLEY. You don't.

JASON. I don't?

HARLEY. I got to thinkin'.

JASON. When?

HARLEY. Later. I really want to put up with all that... that—

JASON. Work...

HARLEY. ...to get a girl? And I mean *come on*: A black and white painting is God?

JASON. I don't think so.

HARLEY. I know so.

JASON. That's so.

HARLEY. I got my integrity, don't you know. *(Pause. Both place cards on the house of cards.)*

JASON. So once was enough, Harley?

HARLEY. I wouldn't go so far to say it was enough.

JASON. How 'bout sufficient?

HARLEY *(pause)*. Yeah...sufficient. *(House of cards collapses as HARLEY deposits final card.)*

BLACKOUT

SPLIT ENDS
By Kerri Kochanski

CHARACTERS

ERIN: 15. Long brown hair. Confident. Does not take any crap. Marches to her own drum.
TANYA: 15. Long hair, but not as long as Erin's. Has a fashionable haircut in the "current" all-American style. Worries about what others think. Insecure. Somewhat demanding.

TIME: Now.
PLACE: Anywhere.

AT RISE: *ERIN, her long hair flipped over her face, is picking at the ends of her strands, splicing off her split ends. TANYA stands watching.*

ERIN. Long one… *(She peels off an end.)* Short one… *(She peels off another one. With concentration, plucking and peeling off—)* Dam-aged one…
TANYA. You're leaving your ends on the ground. *(ERIN continues, oblivious.)* I said you're leaving your—
ERIN. —I know what you said. *(ERIN flips her strands away from her face, revealing her face.)* I don't care… *(ERIN flips the hair back over her face, resuming. TANYA is worried, adamant.)*
TANYA. But people could slip…! People could slip and fall—

51

ERIN *(pointing, not believing)*. —on *my* strands... On my strands sitting there... *(ERIN resumes.)* There's not enough...

TANYA *(looks at the pile)*. Hair...? There is hair... *(Pointing to pile.)* There... Is a *heap*... *(She becomes disgusted.)* Of—

ERIN. —follicles...

TANYA. Yes...

ERIN. Of dead skin cells...

TANYA *(becoming freaked)*. Umm-hmm...

ERIN. Of things you have to part with... Sometimes you *have* to part with the old cells... So you can grow new ones... *(Smoothing her hair, sensually.)* New lines of hair... Covering you... Caressing your—

TANYA *(freaked)*. —I think you have a little *too* much. A little *too* much hair. *(Beat.)* I think you're into your hair too much. I think you need to do other things—

ERIN. —other things.

TANYA. Be*sides* split ends. You need to get out into the world, and do *other things*—

ERIN. —I like doing this... *(ERIN flips her hair over her face again and resumes splitting her ends.)* Besides, other things don't give me pleasure... Not as much... Not as much as—

TANYA. —pulling your hair—

ERIN *(flipping her hair up angrily)*. —I'm *groom*ing... What I'm doing is *groom*ing myself... Animals and monkeys groom... Animals and monkeys—

TANYA. —are not humans. They don't have other things to do. They don't have other *things. (She moves away, imagining. Suggesting—)* Like cheerleading and basketball. *(Beat.)* Don't you want to go out and *do* something...? Don't you want to go out and—

ERIN. —no... *(She flips her hair over her head and begins again.)*

TANYA. So you're just going to sit there... You're just going to sit there and—

ERIN. —yes... *(Beat.)* It doesn't mean you have to though... Sit here...

TANYA. I'm not sitting...

ERIN. Well, hanging around then... You don't have to hang around...

TANYA. I'm not hanging... I'm considering...

ERIN. Considering hanging around...?

TANYA. Considering whether or not... *(She is frustrated.)* Whether or not...

ERIN *(slightly annoyed).* If you don't want to hang around with me anymore, Tanya, just say it. I mean, I'm a big girl. I can take care of it. I can take care of my hair. I could take care of your hair too if you wanted me to—

TANYA. —I don't want you to touch my hair—

ERIN. —it was just a thought... If you wanted to do something... If you wanted to do something together—

TANYA. —I don't want my hair pulled—

ERIN. —I could braid it... I wouldn't have to pull anything off— I could just braid it... Although if you had split ends—

TANYA *(grabbing up her ends).* —I don't *have* split ends... *(She looks at her ends.)* They're perfect... *(Giving it to her.)* My ends... Are perfect...

ERIN *(flipping her hair back over her face).* Then maybe you should become a cheerleader...

TANYA. Cheerleaders don't *have* to have perfect hair... *(Beat.)* Some fake it... Some have perms...

ERIN. I don't have a perm—

TANYA *(getting frustrated)*. —well maybe you should get one… Make…some kind of change…

ERIN *(flipping hair off face)*. If you don't like who I am…

TANYA. I like who you are Erin, I do, but—

ERIN. —you should accept me…

TANYA. Accepting you and dealing with you are—

ERIN *(aggressively)*. —What…

TANYA. It's just…

(TANYA doesn't answer. ERIN grows annoyed.)

ERIN. I'm *wait*ing…

TANYA. You just don't need to do this, you know. To pick at your hair—to end it. To have these ends scattered across the ground. People don't need to *see* these ends. To walk *over* these ends. To walk *over* and *over* these ends. *(She turns to her.)* We've been through this before Erin—

ERIN. —and you keep coming back. You know you just keep coming back. And I don't understand it. If you don't want to be friends with me—

TANYA. —I *do* want to be friends with you—

ERIN *(strongly)*. —well maybe I don't want to be friends with *you*. You know, there's too much pressure. To take care of myself. To take care of my hair. To have you wondering what I do with my hair. To have you yelling at me to not do this or that to my hair. It is *my* hair… And if you don't like looking at it… *(She gets an idea.)* You know, maybe I should chop it off. That's it. I'll chop it off—

TANYA *(relieved)*. —that would be a good idea.

ERIN *(having tricked her)*. But then you'd like that, wouldn't you. *(Getting up.)* And I'm *not* going to do things for you, Tanya. *(Pointing downward.)* If I want to sit here and pick at my hair, then *that* is what I am going to do. Not you, or my mother, or anyone else can tell me what to do. I do what I want to do. It is *my body*. And if you can't get over that then you're just going to have to go somewhere else and find some other person to bug. Bug with your ideas of things. Bug with your demands. Not everyone wants to be a cheerleader or basketball player. Not everyone is good at being a cheerleader or basketball player. Some types of people just want to *be*. One of those people is *me*. One of those people is content to just sit here and pick off her split ends. Not go to the store and get a haircut and have everything be all blunt-cut and nice. I can do it myself! I can take care of myself! I can do what *I* want to do. And I can eat pop rocks too if I want to—

TANYA. —I never said that you couldn't eat—

ERIN. —you said I "shouldn't"! But who cares about pop rocks!? The point is— *(Beat.)* You need to go find something for yourself to do. With*out* me. Without my help... You need to find something that makes you happy on your own. *(Done saying her peace, she drops to the floor. Flips her hair over her face. Resumes picking her ends. TANYA is intrigued, can't understand it.)*

TANYA. You really like splitting that...? *(ERIN continues, ignoring her. TANYA begins to concede.)* Well, if you really like splitting that... *(TANYA begins to feel awkward, uncomfortable.)* Well, I guess I'll leave you alone then... *(TANYA is reluctant to leave but doesn't feel comfortable staying.)* Well, I guess I'll leave you alone... *(She tries to move but is still reluctant. Feels bad. Suddenly, she begins to explain—)* I'm not a bad person... *(Beat.)* It's just—

ERIN *(flipping her hair off her face).* —go find yourself something to do. Something to do that makes yourself happy. Some *one…*

(ERIN flips her hair over her face. TANYA stands there, ill at ease. TANYA puts a hand on her hair and smooths it distractedly. After a while, noticing that she is smoothing her hair, TANYA takes a look at it. Looks at the ends, and is not interested in picking at them. They are perfect. Beginning to fall into somewhat of a daze, TANYA begins braiding two strands. Finished with those, she begins braiding two more strands. Becoming relaxed and mesmerized by the action and the rhythm, TANYA begins to braid two more strands. Intrigued by this newfound activity, TANYA continues to braid. After a while, ERIN moves the hair from her face and sees that TANYA is still there. ERIN realizes that TANYA has found something to do. ERIN doesn't care, or not care. ERIN simply flips her hair over her face and continues to split off her ends. TANYA continues to braid.)

BLACKOUT

GRANNIE'S DESTINATION
By Robin Rice Lichtig

CHARACTERS

ZOE (pronounced "zo-ee"): 12.
CHARLIE: Her twin.

TIME: The present. The twins have learned of their parents' plan to put their grandmother into an old-age home.
PLACE: The yard of their home in rural Massachusetts.

AT RISE: *ZOE and CHARLIE are in deep conversation.*

ZOE. She had a destination.
CHARLIE. She was lost.
ZOE. She knew.
CHARLIE. She forgot.
ZOE. She doesn't want to go.
CHARLIE. Did she say?
ZOE. She won't.
CHARLIE. She has to.
ZOE. Why?
CHARLIE. It's the best thing.
ZOE. *They* think.
CHARLIE. They know.
ZOE. They think they know.
CHARLIE. You know better? No.
ZOE. She's *my* grandmother.
CHARLIE. She's Mom's *mother*.

57

ZOE. She's not Dad's anything.

CHARLIE. Mother-in-law.

ZOE. He doesn't have any of her blood in his veins. I do.

CHARLIE. I do too and I—

ZOE *(interrupting)*. I love her more.

CHARLIE. I did first.

ZOE. More.

CHARLIE. First.

ZOE. Seventy-two seconds. Big deal.

CHARLIE. She's not your exclusive grannie.

ZOE. You didn't even want to look for her. They had to peel you off your stupid computer.

CHARLIE. Who found her? Me.

ZOE. You want somebody deciding what you have to do when you're old and can't walk so good?

CHARLIE. I'll never be that old.

ZOE. Seventy-two seconds before me you will be.

CHARLIE. What's the point?

ZOE. It's her life.

CHARLIE. She'll do it again.

ZOE. I'm going to help her.

CHARLIE. Like you helped Blueback?

ZOE. What about Blueback?

CHARLIE. You let him out.

ZOE. So what?

CHARLIE. It's an example of what happens when you let birdbrains—

ZOE. Charlie Fogerty!

CHARLIE. It's a fact.

ZOE. Grannie does not have a small brain.

CHARLIE. You opened his cage and the window and he flew out and—

ZOE. He wanted out.

CHARLIE. ...and walked off across the snow like a penguin. A parakeet thinking he's a penguin.

ZOE. He could be okay.

CHARLIE. He's dead.

ZOE. Maybe not.

CHARLIE. D-E-A-D.

ZOE. Grannie's not a bird.

CHARLIE. When you get that old your brain dries out
and shrinks up like a Grapenut.

ZOE. I love Grapenuts. Grannie loves Grapenuts.

CHARLIE. You can't chew Grapenuts with old teeth.

ZOE. It's all the way over in Pittsfield.

CHARLIE. You can visit.

ZOE. I can't walk there. I can't go every day.

CHARLIE. You don't now.

ZOE. I could.

CHARLIE. Grow up, Zoe. Everything can't always be
how you like it.

ZOE. What about her?

CHARLIE. Where are you going?

ZOE. None of your beeswax.

CHARLIE. You'll be late for supper.

ZOE. I'm not hungry.

CHARLIE. I'm not making excuses for you.

ZOE. You have a computer for a heart, Charlie Fogerty.

CHARLIE. Mom's making spaghetti.

ZOE. I prefer SpaghettiOs.

CHARLIE. Oh. I s'pose Grannie's opening a can of
SpaghettiOs and invited you and not me.

ZOE. Me and Grannie have a plan—so there! *(ZOE sticks
her tongue out, exits.)*

CHARLIE. What plan? Wait up! What plan?

BLACKOUT

WEDDING TALK
By Edward Mast

CHARACTERS

MURASAKI: A teenage woman.
TONO: A teenage woman. Murasaki's servant.
AWOI: An older woman.
VOICE OF A SERVANT

TIME: The past.
PLACE: A palace in medieval Japan.

AT RISE: *TONO and MURASAKI are admiring a length of white silk.*

TONO. Not all this.
MURASAKI. All this. And all left over from my wedding gown.
TONO. No.
MURASAKI. Yes, left over.
TONO. So beauuutiful.
MURASAKI. And a belt of embroidered gold for the sash.
TONO. He is so generous.
MURASAKI *(improvises a poem).*
    his generous hand
    a waving flag declaring
    a so giving heart
  (Pause.)
Is it true that Genji won the Battle of Soonjo Bridge?

60

TONO. They say he did. When he was younger. I wasn't there.

MURASAKI. Everyone says so.

TONO. I am told you can read it in history books.

MURASAKI. I'll find those books and read them. Genji has met the Emperor. We'll travel all over the empire, we'll meet all the famous lords and their ladies.

TONO. You will.

MURASAKI. We'll travel outside the empire.

TONO. You will?

MURASAKI. Why not? To the Manchu country. Farther. Who knows?

TONO. Why would you go there?

MURASAKI. Don't you want to see the whole world?

TONO. Not especially. I'd be happy just to be married to someone like you're gonna marry.

MURASAKI. You will.

TONO. No I won't. I'll be an unmarried toy for gentlemen all my life. That's my place. Unless some dashing bandit kidnaps me.

MURASAKI. Then you'd see the world.

TONO. I suppose.

MURASAKI. Maybe you can come see the world with me.

TONO. I can?

MURASAKI. Why not? I'll need a personal woman, won't I? To dress me and feed me and keep the fires going in my rooms, isn't that right?

TONO. Of course.

MURASAKI. And besides, we're friends.

TONO. We are?

MURASAKI. Aren't you my friend?

TONO. Well sure, but you don't have to be *my* friend.

MURASAKI. But I *want* to. Don't you see? I'm not like those other ladies. I haven't been rich all my life like them. *(Whispers.)* I grew up in a teeny little house.

TONO. You did?

MURASAKI. Two rooms. Didn't you?

TONO. Yeah.

MURASAKI. See? I'm the same as you. I just got a stroke of wonderful fate, and now I can have all the things I want, and I never have to build a fire again, but that doesn't mean we can't be friends.

TONO. Really?

MURASAKI. You're my newest friend. You're the first friend I've made here in my new home.

TONO. Except your husband, of course.

MURASAKI. Of course. And we're not really friends yet. That happens after the wedding. Doesn't it?

TONO. I guess so. I hope so.

MURASAKI. Me too.

TONO. What's important is you're happy.

MURASAKI. What's important is that weak-in-the-knees feeling, you know, that romance.

TONO. Does Genji give that to you?

MURASAKI. Well not yet, but he will, won't he?

TONO. Do you like his gray hair?

MURASAKI. Of course, don't you?

TONO. I suppose. He's kind of old.

MURASAKI. He's not so old.

TONO. Fifty-two years.

MURASAKI. He's mature. Gray hair gives him dignity. He's not some boy. When he visits I can hear his footsteps all down the road, like an emperor himself.

TONO. And now you're his bride.

MURASAKI. Bride to be.

TONO. That's the best part. Better than later.

MURASAKI. I don't think so. I think being wife to the great Genji will be paradise.

TONO. Where were you when he saw you from afar?

MURASAKI. Oh, you know, in a meadow near my house.

TONO. Running around outside?

MURASAKI. Not running, but outside.

TONO. We never go outside here.

MURASAKI. Never?

TONO. Into the garden sometimes. But when we leave the house we go in carriages with blinds across the windows.

MURASAKI. Why?

TONO. When you live in a nobleman's house, you're not supposed to be seen by anyone else.

MURASAKI. That's not a rule, is it?

TONO. Sort of.

MURASAKI. Oh. Well. That will be fine. We have a huuuge garden, don't we? *(A knock.)* Yes?

VOICE *(offstage)*. My Lady Awoi visits.

MURASAKI. Who?

VOICE. My Lady Awoi visits.

MURASAKI *(whispers)*. Who's that?

TONO *(whispers)*. You don't know?

AWOI *(offstage, impatient)*. The young lady will receive me.

(MURASAKI and TONO leap into their poses as AWOI enters. AWOI is handsome and magnificently dressed, wearing a half-mask to designate high status. She steps in, looks skeptically at MURASAKI. Silence.)

AWOI. You are this…Murasaki.

MURASAKI. I am. *(TONO nudges her.)* Your Ladyship.

AWOI. Your courtesy does you credit, young lady. You are pretty. *(Pause.)* I say you are pretty.

MURASAKI. Thank your Ladyship.

AWOI. I hope you are…patient and…companionable also, as well as hardworking when that time comes.

MURASAKI. I hope to be, your Ladyship.

AWOI. I desire you to know that I bear you no animosity. This is not, after all, your fault.

MURASAKI. I fail to understand, your Ladyship.

AWOI. Mm. Of course you do. Well. I was instructed not to come here, but it is my duty. The duty of one in my place. To uhh. To make you welcome. Into my Lord Genji's…family.

MURASAKI. Thank your Ladyship. What is my Lady's relation to the Lord Genji?

AWOI. Is your question impertinent?

MURASAKI. No, your Ladyship.

AWOI. I would hope not. But you must be either impertinent or ignorant. Which shall it be?

MURASAKI. If seeking information means ignorance, my Lady, then I am ignorant on a regular basis, your Ladyship.

AWOI *(glares at her a moment)*. Did you not hear me announced as the Lady Awoi?

MURASAKI. Yes, your Ladyship.

AWOI. The Lady Awoi? Lord Genji's wife?

MURASAKI. I beg your pardon? Wife? *(TONO nudges her.)* Your Ladyship?

AWOI. Yes. Wife.

MURASAKI. With many pardons, your Ladyship, I am to be married to the Lord Genji tomorrow.

AWOI. You surprise me. Has no one talked to you? Perhaps that is why I was discouraged from this visit. I am the wife of Lord Genji. Your ceremony tomorrow, if we may call it so, is a formal process to make legal the introduction of secondary wives into the household.

MURASAKI. I am to be his second wife?

AWOI. His fourth wife, actually. None of the others have called on you? That's unfortunate. They are usually possessed of better manners. Perhaps they were forbidden as well.

MURASAKI. There are two others?

AWOI. I am sorry to be the bearer of this disagreeable news to you. Yes, there are two others, as well as myself. You will have a distinct advantage, however. You are still young. All of us started young, but time has passed. It has passed for our Lord Genji as well, and as his hair has turned more gray, he has developed a taste for extra wives to make him feel young again and not so gray. Do you see now?

MURASAKI. Yes. *(TONO nudges.)* Your Ladyship.

AWOI. Hm. I think you are genuinely surprised by this. The shock will wear off. We do not have much choice in these matters. I hope for your sake that the arrangement agrees with you. It does seem to suit some people. Good day, Fourth Wife. *(AWOI leaves without bowing.)*

TONO. You really didn't know?

MURASAKI. How was I supposed to? Why didn't you tell me?

TONO. I thought you knew. They told me not to mention it, but I thought we were just being polite. She wasn't supposed to come here.

MURASAKI. Who told her not to?

TONO. Lord Genji, I think.

MURASAKI. Lord Genji told her not to?

TONO. I think so. It's not so bad, you know.

MURASAKI. "I hope the arrangement agrees with you." It does *not* agree with me. He can look elsewhere for his many spare brides.

TONO. Uh...

MURASAKI. What?

TONO. You said he gave gifts to your parents, right?

MURASAKI. So?

TONO. So really, you belong to him now.

MURASAKI. I do?

TONO *(nods)*. You'll have a nice life. All the gowns and jewels you want. Sweets to eat all day. No work to do.

MURASAKI. Sounds easy, doesn't it.

TONO. Sure does.

MURASAKI. We'll see.

BLACKOUT

THE MAKEOVER
By Rosemary McLaughlin

CHARACTERS

SUE: A teenager.
DEE: Her teenage cousin.

TIME: The present.
PLACE: Dee's bedroom.

AT RISE: *SUE and DEE are seated on the floor; SUE is dressed in a Catholic school uniform; DEE is in a sweatshirt and jeans.*

DEE. Again.
SUE. I'm not doing this anymore. This is a ridiculous game for us to do at our age.
DEE. Once more!
SUE. I've got homework to do.
DEE. I said, one more time.
DEE & SUE. Ring around the rosy... Pocket full of posy... Ashes, ashes... We all fall down.
(They fall; DEE gets up first and pushes SUE down; DEE laughs.)
SUE. Cut it out, *Dee*. Let go of me.
(Angrily, SUE grabs hold of DEE's leg and pulls her down.)
DEE. What the hell do you think you're doing?
(Jumps on top of SUE.)

67

SUE. Get off me! *(She gets free.)* What are you? Some kind of animal? If you don't like me, just leave me alone.

DEE. Who said I didn't like you? We always used to play together when we were kids.

SUE. I know. The scabs are still healing.

DEE. Wanna play stoop ball?

SUE. I'm going to study now. *(She does so.)*

DEE. And does Aunt Carol give my little cousin Suzie milk and cookies when she comes home with good grades?

SUE. Jealous.

DEE. No way! Wanna hang out on the roof?

SUE. What for?

DEE. It'd be fun. Wanna smoke?

SUE. Yuck.

DEE. For crying out loud, you don't even know what I was gonna ask you to smoke!

SUE. Whatever it is I don't want it.

DEE *(glancing at SUE's papers)*. That's not homework. *(SUE tries to cover them up.)* Who's that from? Your boyfriend?
(Snatches letter from SUE.)

SUE. Give that back to me!

DEE. Suzie's got a boyfriend!

SUE. You've got no right to read that!

DEE. Says who?

SUE. It's a federal offense! You can go to jail!

DEE. "Dear Susan, *how* I enjoyed canoeing on the lake with you this summer." A little lakeside action, huh, Sue? I didn't think you had it in you.

SUE. Give it to me!

DEE. "Remember the day we planted the marigolds? They're still going strong keeping the aphids off the tomatoes." *(Pause.)* No wonder you don't want to talk about him. *(She allows SUE to grab the letter back.)* He lives far away? Sue. Where does he live?

SUE. You had your fun.

DEE. Tell me about him.

SUE. I have work to do.

DEE. Answer me.

SUE. Why don't you go outside and play or something? *(In reply, DEE swats SUE's books off table.)* Thanks a lot. *(DEE kicks books away.)* It's from my cousin, OK? Not a boyfriend.

DEE. What cousin? I'm your cousin.

SUE. The other side of the family.

(She approaches her books; DEE blocks her path.)

DEE. How come I never heard of them?

SUE. Uncle Frank, Aunt Marge, Sheilah and her big brothers who are married. I just met them all. They live in Ohio.

DEE. That's a pretty drippy letter coming from a cousin. What did you do? Fall in love?

SUE. When I went there in July. I had a very good time.

DEE. What's his name?

SUE *(with growing exasperation and volume)*. Her name is Sheilah! She's in the same grade as me and she belongs to the 4-H Club! Her specialty is canning and preserving fruit!

DEE *(sings)*.

Sue and Sheilah sitting in a tree
K-i-s-s-i-n-g!

(SUE reaches for her books, DEE plants her foot on them.)

I didn't say you could have them back.

SUE. Too bad. I said so.

DEE. Just who do you think's in charge here?

SUE. Your mother.

(SUE again reaches for her books; DEE plants foot on her hand.)

DEE. She's not here. Who's in charge?

SUE. Nobody!

DEE. Who?

SUE *(struggling to free her hand)*. Get off my hand!

DEE. Who's in charge?

SUE. You are! Get off!

DEE. You better start getting along with me.

SUE. You're hurting me!

(DEE lifts foot; SUE sobs.)

DEE. Oh, come on. It can't hurt that much. Don't be such a baby. Let me see. *(Tries to look at SUE's hand, but SUE pulls it away.)* It's not even turning color. But your face sure is. Jeez, are you red!

SUE. Oh, no! Am I? My mother's going to know I was crying.

DEE. You're right. We'll have to fix that. *(Goes for her pocketbook.)*

SUE. What are you going to do?

DEE. Don't worry. I'm gonna make you look beautiful. This lipstick'll go good with your hair. *(DEE applies makeup liberally.)*

SUE. Who cares about that? My hair wasn't crying.

DEE. Right now you look like a Chinese apple all over: eyes, lips, everything. Just be glad you got the Picasso of Maybelline putting out the fire.

SUE. Easy does it or my mother's going to have a fit. She says I'm too young for makeup. I don't want to get yelled at.

DEE. Better you than me, kid.

SUE. Are you sure you know what you're doing with this stuff?

DEE. Are you kidding? I wear it all the time. You ought to see yourself. I'm creating something here.

SUE. You're creating trouble, that's all.

DEE. I am transforming you from a crybaby into a cover girl. Your mother'll die.

SUE. She better not!

DEE. Hold still. Are you like this at school? No wonder nobody likes you.

SUE. Then how come I was elected class vice president?

DEE. I never see you hang out with anybody.

SUE. If you're so popular where are all your friends now?

DEE. I had to put them away. Snuff 'em. You can find their body parts in the Meadowlands. If you dare.
(SUE listens intently, then reaches for the mascara, swiping it across DEE's face.)

SUE. *En garde!*
(DEE, shocked, leaps to her feet, studies this new side of her cousin then gleefully grabs makeup with both hands.)

DEE. *En garde* yourself! *(They duel with cosmetics, playing rough. DEE loses her balance, falling onto her back. SUE pounces on top of her, pinning her down. She holds the lipstick triumphantly over DEE's face, poised for a final coup de grace.)* You are so dead if you do it. (SUE continues to hold DEE and the lipstick in place.)* I mean it.

SUE *(mimicking).* I mean it.

(DEE studies SUE as if seeing her for the first time; she laughs. SUE laughs, then swipes her own face with the lipstick. DEE pauses, startled, then laughs. SUE laughs, rolls off DEE. They howl with laughter, lying on the floor.)

BLACKOUT

THE GRETCHEN WORM
By Max Bush

CHARACTERS

KAT: 15.
DOUGLAS: 18.

TIME: The present. Saturday afternoon in early June.
PLACE: A park near a duck pond.

AT RISE: *DOUGLAS waits by the duck pond fence. KAT enters.*

KAT. Hey, Douglas.
DOUGLAS. Hi, Kat.
KAT. What you doin'?
DOUGLAS. Waiting for somebody. What are you doing?
KAT. Can I stand with you a while?
DOUGLAS. Sure.
  (She stands up against him, which makes him move away from her.)
KAT. I like them ducks. Is that why you're here, you like the ducks?
DOUGLAS. Sure, I like ducks.
KAT. I like the *pretty* ducks. How long you been out here, today, Douglas?
DOUGLAS. Half hour. Why?
KAT. What way'd you come into the park?
DOUGLAS. By the statues. Why?

KAT. You ain't seen my mom out here, have you?

DOUGLAS. No. I haven't seen your mom. Are you supposed to meet her here?

(Short silence. KAT leans over to kiss DOUGLAS, DOUGLAS recoils.)

KAT. How come you don't like me, Douglas?

DOUGLAS. I like you.

KAT. You know what I mean.

DOUGLAS. Ah, I got a girlfriend already, Kat.

KAT. Oh, that neighbor girl. She's young for you, ain't she?

DOUGLAS. Yeah, well, I still like her. It's not my fault Gretchen's fourteen.

KAT. How come we never hooked up? I'm fifteen.

DOUGLAS. Too old! *(He laughs.)*

KAT. But I'm just as—

DOUGLAS. And you're way older than fifteen!

KAT. Yeah, yeah, I know what you mean.

DOUGLAS. Yeah, you know what I mean.

KAT. Yeah, I know what you mean.

DOUGLAS. Yeah, so, I even named my new invention after Gretchen.

KAT. That computer thing?

DOUGLAS. No, the other one.

KAT. You got something else?

DOUGLAS. Yeah, oh, yeah, it's something I've been working on for years.

KAT. And you named it after her.

DOUGLAS. Gretchen's good for people. And she's just good for everything. She'd be good for me.

KAT. Is she—

DOUGLAS. If she'd just like me back!

KAT. She don't like you back? And you named your invention after her? That's cold. What is it?

DOUGLAS. I haven't even told her, yet. But I'm going to. No, I haven't told her yet. But, if you won't tell anybody, I'll tell you.

KAT. I won't say anything.

DOUGLAS. I invented, well, I bred, I've been breeding, a new kind of...worm.

KAT. A worm. That's your invention? A damn worm?

DOUGLAS. Well, it's not a damn worm, it's The Gretchen Worm.

KAT. Hey, Douglas?

DOUGLAS. Yeah?

KAT. Don't name any inventions after me.

DOUGLAS. No, you see, it goes into landfills—the world is filling up with garbage and it doesn't rot, see? Bacteria isn't fast enough, regular worms are better but are too slow; and you don't want to burn all that garbage, so I took different kinds of worms and put them together to...I bred a worm that would break the garbage down two—almost three—times faster. They'll make the world a better place—like Gretchen. Gretchen makes the world a better place.

KAT. Man, you love her.

DOUGLAS. Yeah, but don't tell her that.

KAT. I guess I shoulda known you better when I was younger—when I was twelve! Ain't nobody naming squat after me.

DOUGLAS. Ah, you'll find a boyfriend. He'll name his hot car after you. What are you doing out here anyway?

KAT. I was looking for my mom. She didn't come home last night. She's probably locked up again. I'm going to lose my godforsaken mind. I told her, "If you ever need something, I'll get it for you. If you ever need to do something, I'll do it for you." And we had good conversations lately, too. I told her I did not give up on her. She promised she didn't give up on me. We went to the beach last week, for Christ sake, and went swimming. I did her hair, too—bought her a big pretty new barrette with shiny stones in it. I've been home every night for a month. I told her, "Stay out of the park at night and I will too. Just come home and stay out of that park 'cause you know the place is like hell with temptations for you. Got rats and disease at night." Damn, she don't listen. She told me she'd come home at night. She lied. I hate lies. Have I ever lied to you, Douglas? *(He indicates no.)* Damn that's right! That's 'cause there ain't nothing worse than lies. She's probably on E. That stuff don't leave you alone for three days. And then she don't eat. And then she gets stupid. She's going to jail again, unless I find her.

DOUGLAS. Whatever happened to your dad?

KAT. Who? *(She laughs.)* Who?

DOUGLAS. I got it.

KAT. If I ever found him I'd kick his worthless ass. Oh my God, my head is spinning—I did not give up on her! I didn't yell at her. I told her to stay away from here. She doesn't have to hide from me like this!

DOUGLAS. I'm sorry I can't help you look, I'm waiting for Gretchen.

KAT. Yeah, that's all right, my ma's probably not here anymore, anyway. Maybe she's home.

DOUGLAS. Yeah.

KAT. Maybe she went home after I left. Maybe she went out the other way.

DOUGLAS. Yeah, and I'm waiting for Gretchen. She's meeting me here.

KAT. Yeah, OK, wait here. I got to stay with you anyway.

DOUGLAS. Why?

KAT. We got to talk to you, Douglas.

DOUGLAS. Who does? About what?

KAT. It's all right. It's all right. I got some friends who'd like to meet you, 'cause I told them good things about you, my brother.

DOUGLAS. Those bangers?

KAT. They're teaching me their codes, they're lettin' me in, Douglas, and it's...it's good... It's good.

DOUGLAS. What's good about it?

KAT. I told them about you. About your inventions and your computers and—your picture-in-the-paper!—and they got all excited, man. Tonya especially—you've seen Tonya—wooo, was she hot. They never got that excited about me.

DOUGLAS. About me?

KAT. Yeah, so—

DOUGLAS. They don't know me, do they?

KAT. I said I told them about you! So they want to meet you, they want to talk with you.

DOUGLAS. About what?

KAT. You should see the difference it makes. No one messes with me, anymore, and I ain't even *in* yet.

DOUGLAS. No one messes with me, Kat. No one even knows I'm here.

KAT. They talk to me like I'm somebody. And J.T. and Tonya don't lie to me. They never lie to me and tell me they'll be there for me and then not show up.

DOUGLAS. I never lie to you.

KAT. That's right. That's what I told them.

DOUGLAS. What did Tonya say?

KAT. Ah, I'll let her tell you herself, 'cause I can't talk like her. I don't look like her, either, do I?

DOUGLAS. You look fine, Kat.

KAT. What you got to do, anyway? Stand around waiting for a girlfriend who don't care about you, who ain't comin'? Well, Tonya's comin', and J.T. *(Pointing off.)* —there they are now—'cause they're excited about you. You talk to them, Douglas, straight up, and tell them what you want. I know they'll listen, and I know they'll do what they say they're gonna do.

BLACKOUT

THE MIRROR
By Claudia Haas

CHARACTERS

ANNA: 15. Reveals all the growing pains, foibles and in-
securities of an adolescent girl.
MIRROR: A more secure version of Anna. Should reflect
Anna but does not necessarily need to be a carbon copy
of her.

TIME: A weekday, morning.
PLACE: Anna's bedroom.

AT RISE: *ANNA is seen getting ready for school. Bed un-
made, shoes off, she has her jeans and T-shirt on, she's
inspecting herself. Off to one side is the "MIRROR"
played by another actress. You may use an actual
frame or not—your choice. The other actress may or
may not look like ANNA—again your choice—but the
MIRROR must accurately reflect ANNA's movements.
ANNA's hair is flopped over her face as she seeks to
"hide" herself.*

ANNA *(turning around and looking at herself from all
sides)*. Getting tight! *(She sucks in her stomach with a
big breath.)* Almost time for the fat jeans.
MIRROR. Here it comes. Anna's morning's litany of what
horrible things she sees in the mirror. She's just fine!
I'm fine. When will she see that?

ANNA. Maybe the mirror is like the camera—maybe it adds ten pounds.

MIRROR. You don't need to lose weight. Please don't go back on that tangent.

ANNA. I have to lay off the cookies.

MIRROR. You're young! Have a cookie!

ANNA. I will not ever eat another cookie ever, ever again! Today, I will suck in my stomach and just not breathe all day.

MIRROR. And you'll be passed out before you get to the bus stop.

ANNA. Time for the big sweater!

MIRROR. I hate that sweater. You don't need a huge cover-up. *(ANNA puts on the sweater. She is "caught" inside.)* I hate when you do that. This is so uncomfortable. All the twisting and turning... *(ANNA's head pops out.)* There!

ANNA. Finally! Oh no!

MIRROR. Now what?

ANNA. Look at my hair!

MIRROR. I am looking at it. I have no choice. Don't start on the hair. Leave me with something positive this morning.

ANNA. I'll have to put it up. Hide it.

MIRROR. Once the hair is out of the way, she's going to start on her face.

(ANNA goes to put up her hair in a ponytail. As she does that, she comes closer to the MIRROR and screams!)

ANNA. Ahhhh!

MIRROR. What?

ANNA. When did that happen?

MIRROR. What? *Whaat??*

ANNA. This zit! Where did this come from? *(Yelling at MIRROR.)* Go away! *Scram!* Why am I plagued with oily skin?

MIRROR. You're a kid! It's natural. It's tiny. No one cares.

ANNA. Why can't you just once look back at me and show me something...acceptable?

MIRROR. Look! *Look!* There's nothing wrong with you! It's your perception that's off! You look great!

ANNA. A few little chocolate chip cookies and the body wears them like red flags announcing, "Hey everyone, look! Anna's a tub!"

MIRROR. You're fit. You're healthy. Human beings were not made to look like walking twigs.

ANNA. And then there's this mop on my head...

MIRROR. Of shiny, healthy hair.

ANNA. And finally, I am covered with splotchy, oily, coming-up-roses skin!

MIRROR. One little pimple. One tiny, minuscule bump that would never be noticed if you would smile once in a while.

ANNA. I hate the way I look!

MIRROR. And I hate the way you hate the way I look. Every morning, I wake up positive. Then you come over and put down every inch of me. Your ritual of de-tailing what you deem to be my physical failings leaves me thoroughly demoralized. I don't know how you face the day! Smile! Look! *Look! There's nothing wrong with you!* Stop making horrible faces at me all the time... *(As ANNA scowls into the mirror inspecting herself, the MIRROR unhappily has no choice but to scowl back.)* Let me smile! I don't think you've let me smile in weeks! Remember when you were little and you twirled around the room wearing tights on your head...oh, those were fun days.

ANNA. Even when I was little, I hated my hair! I remember putting tights on my head and pretending that they were my actual hair. At least it always stayed in place. How pathetic is that?

MIRROR. It was charming. Those were the good old days. You smiled all the time. We looked pretty.

ANNA *(opening her mouth and inspecting her teeth).* Well, at least I have straight teeth.

MIRROR. There you go. Something affirmative.

ANNA. Of course, it was thousands and thousands of dollars to have my teeth straightened...

MIRROR. But they're straight! *Smile!*

ANNA. Maybe if I spent thousands and thousands of dollars on my body, *that* could look good, also.

MIRROR. *What?*

ANNA. People have their noses done all the time.

MIRROR. Your nose? When did you start hating your nose?

ANNA. And their eyebrows waxed, and their tummies tucked...

MIRROR. Tummies tucked? You're sixteen!

ANNA. I could get my hair highlighted. That only costs about a hundred bucks.

MIRROR. And it will lose its natural shine! Leave your hair alone!

ANNA. I can't stand it!

MIRROR. I can't stand it!

ANNA. I wish my teeth were whiter.

MIRROR. Wait a minute! I thought you liked your teeth! Don't start putting down the teeth now! Leave me with some shred of self-esteem.

ANNA. It's no use. I should just stay in bed all day so nobody has to look at me.

MIRROR. Oh. This is no good. Come here. *(ANNA comes closer to the MIRROR.)* Closer. *(ANNA does so.)* Now, listen to me. You look fine. Better than fine. You look great! You are the picture of health, youth and beauty! You have all your fingers and toes and your eyes are in the right place and a light comes on when you smile.

ANNA. I'll never look like those girls in the magazines.

MIRROR. Those girls don't look like those girls in the magazines. They are photos! Retouched! You are a human being! At the cusp of your life! Celebrate! Celebrate who you are! *Please!* Look at me! Really look.

ANNA. I'm hot. If I wear this sweater all day, I'm just going to sweat and be gross.

MIRROR *(getting extremely frustrated)*. Now, we have to go through the sweater thing again…which will mess her hair…

ANNA. It's going.

(ANNA takes off the sweater, fighting it to get her head out. MIRROR does the same.)

MIRROR. Okay, back to square one.

ANNA. What can I do to cover up my body?

MIRROR. *Don't do anything!*

ANNA. So, do I leave the hair down to hide my face or put my hair up to hide my hair?

MIRROR. Leave your hair down and *get it off your face!* Show off your eyes! They say the eyes are the mirror to your soul.

ANNA. Maybe if I add a belt, it will pull everything together. *(Pause.)* Of course, it'll call attention to my waist and make it look bigger.

MIRROR. I've had it! *Had it!* Do you hear? You have all these gifts! You play sports, you sing! You're fit. You're beautiful! Please, let me start one day feeling beautiful!

ANNA. Maybe a little mascara…

MIRROR. Okay, but just a little. And don't poke me in the eye with the wand.

ANNA *(applying mascara)*. There! At least I'm not totally horrendous. Some blush. *(She applies a little blush.)*

MIRROR. Go easy. You want to enhance not cover up.

ANNA. I guess I could be worse.

MIRROR. While that's not the most life-affirming statement I have ever heard, it is a step in the right direction.

ANNA. I don't know. When I take myself apart, I hate everything about me.

MIRROR. So, don't take yourself apart.

ANNA. But when I look at everything put together… *(ANNA steps back.)*

MIRROR. Yes?

ANNA. It kind of works…

MIRROR. *Yes!*

ANNA. In a haphazard sort of way…

MIRROR. Come on, you can do better than that.

ANNA. I mean, if my nose was any smaller my face would be out of proportion.

MIRROR. There you go. I'm feeling better already.

ANNA. Oh! Running late. Better go! Where's my backpack?

MIRROR. In the hallway. Remember? You packed it last night and brought it into the hall.

ANNA. I left it in the hall. Another busy day. Okay! Final check! Hair?

MIRROR. Get it out of your face!! How can you work at school with your hair all over?

ANNA *(sticking it back)*. There. Outfit?

MIRROR. Cute. You look really cute.

ANNA. It's comfortable. It'll be a long day. I need comfort. Skin?

MIRROR. Don't get off track.

ANNA. Oh well, I've lived with a pimple before and I guess I can again. Makeup?

MIRROR. Nice. Understated.

ANNA. Don't have time to put any more on.

MIRROR. There's a blessing.

ANNA. Well, I've looked better. But then again, I've certainly looked worse. I'm out of here. See you later. *(ANNA runs off.)*

MIRROR. Have a great day!

BLACKOUT

BRICKS
By Lucinda McDermott

Bricks was produced as part of City Theatre's "Summer Shorts Festival 2004," performing at the Ring Theatre, Coral Gables and at the Broward Center for the Performing Arts in Ft. Lauderdale, Florida.

CHARACTERS

JULIA: 15.
ROBBIE: 17. Julia's brother, mentally challenged.

TIME: The present.
PLACE: The kitchen or dining room in their grandmother's home.

AT RISE: *JULIA is methodically going through a stack of floral cards one by one, making a list of people who have sent flowers to their grandmother's funeral. ROBBIE is building a house out of Leggoes.*

JULIA. "Mr. and Mrs. Donald Ferris." Ferris. Donald Ferris. Ferris. Robbie, does the name "Donald Ferris" ring a bell?
ROBBIE. Joanahleelah.
JULIA. 'scuse me?
ROBBIE. Joanahleelah. The Cookie Lady. At church.
JULIA. Joan. Joan Ferris.
ROBBIE. Joanahleelah—

JULIA & ROBBIE. The Cookie Lady.

ROBBIE. At church.

JULIA. Right. Joan and Donald Ferris. They gave the lilies.

ROBBIE. What Julia? They gave the what?

JULIA. Lilies. The big white flowers.

ROBBIE. Li—leeeeeeees.

JULIA. I hate lilies.

ROBBIE. Liiiiiiiiiiiileeeeeeees. Like liiiiiiiillllllllleeeeeees.

JULIA. Flowers of death.

ROBBIE. Nuh-uh, Julia, they're not!

JULIA. Yes, they are, flowers of death. You only see them when somebody dies. I hate them.

ROBBIE. I see 'em at Easter!

JULIA. Yeah, and what's Easter?

ROBBIE. Bunnies and eggs.

JULIA. Jesus died.

ROBBIE. He rose! In the sky! Grandma said! He flew!

JULIA. First he died. Lilies. It's like so obvious. Why wouldn't they be somewhat original and give something a little more subtle. Like the Williams'. *(Holds up card.)* They gave sunflowers! Grandma loved sunflowers.

ROBBIE. When she coming home?

JULIA. Aunt Ila is picking us up tomorrow. We have to have all our stuff packed in the morning. We've been over this.

ROBBIE. You are ignorant. I'm talking about Grandmaaaaaaa.

JULIA. Robbie—

ROBBIE *(sings a song of his own making).*
    I built a house, a nice, nice house
    Where happy people liiiiiiiiiive.

And in my house, this nice, nice house
No badness ever iiiiiiiiisssss.
(*Pause.*)
Grandma is going to love my house. Like it?

JULIA. Where were we this afternoon?

ROBBIE. Don't know.

JULIA. Yes, you do. You greeted people. You were fine. You were norm—you were fine. What's the problem now?

ROBBIE. Look at that! It is six o'clock and that cat has not been fed. Grandma! Zephyrs gone be mad at you!

JULIA. Look at me!

ROBBIE (*singing*).
I built a house, a nice, nice house—

JULIA (*interrupting*). Look at me! (*Tries to grab him.*)

ROBBIE. No.

JULIA. Look at—

ROBBIE. No!

JULIA. Please. Please, Robbie. Look. Don't retreat. Don't go into that nowhere zone of yours. Robbie! You're scaring me. You're scaring me because you're—you're making me think you're…

ROBBIE. What?

JULIA. —crazy!

ROBBIE. I'm retarded.

JULIA. Besides that. No, no, you're not retarded, okay, you are, but we're not supposed to say that anymore we're supposed to say you're—

ROBBIE. Mentally challenged.

JULIA. Yeah. Robbie—

ROBBIE. It is six o'clock! Ding dong! Time to feed the cat! Grandmaaaaaaaaaaaaaaaaa!

JULIA. She is gone!

ROBBIE. Do you see her, Julia? Do you see her? No! Why? She's gone! Duh! Big duh, duh, duh, duh! She's not here, unless she's invisible. Grandma, are you invisible? Of course she's gone, Julia. God, even a retard can figure that one.

JULIA *(tries to work on card list again)*. Where is she, Rob?

ROBBIE. Don't know. Store.

JULIA. Why are you doing this? I can't take this! It's enough dealing with—I'm fifteen years old and in the past three days I've watched my grandmother die, talked to police, picked out a casket, planned—figured out—called people— Robbie. Please. I can't—

ROBBIE. Shut up!

JULIA. Robbie—

ROBBIE. You shut up! You listen to me. It is Zephyr's dinnertime! And Grandma is a little late but she'll apologize and she will be home and take care of us like she has ever since Mom and Daddy flew the plane to heaven.

JULIA. You're my big brother, right?

ROBBIE. Always always always.

JULIA. What does Grandma always tell you about being a big brother?

ROBBIE *(thinks, and remembers)*. Oops. Doo-doo. Ca-ca. Poo-poo. Feces. *(He goes over to his sister and puts his arms around her.)* Julia. Oh, Julia. Something terrible happened. Grandma died.

JULIA *(with relief)*. Yes.

ROBBIE. But don't you worry. It's going to be okay. I'm going to take care of you.

JULIA. You will?

ROBBIE. Uh-huh, because that's my job.

JULIA *(clinging to him)*. Don't leave me again like that, okay? Don't scare me. Please.

ROBBIE. Okay, Julia. Okay.

JULIA. I love you, Robbie.

ROBBIE *(sings)*.

I built a house, a nice, nice house
Where happy people liiiiiiiiiive.
And in my house, this nice, nice house
No badness ever iiiiiiiiissssss.

BLACKOUT

THINKING ABOUT LINCOLN
By Cynthia Mercati

CHARACTERS

MARY
OZZIE

Note: This piece may be performed by one girl and one boy, by two girls, or by two boys.

TIME: Now.
PLACE: A Ferris wheel represented by two folding chairs.

AT RISE: *OZZIE and MARY sit side by side. They are on a Ferris wheel and have just come to a sudden stop. MARY is nervous, anxious to please and given to talking—a lot. She is also dressed like the all-American girl. Her hair, makeup, outfit, purse, shoes, everything about her, screams: Suburbs! Money! Uptight! OZZIE is laid back and works hard at being absolutely, dead-on, cool. Maybe he's a Goth, maybe not, but his appearance screams back at MARY's in total defiance.*

MARY *(looking down, as she babbles nervously)*. Wow, it's really high up here. Did you know it was gonna be so high up here? I don't know if I would've gotten on, if I'd known it was gonna be so high up. It's really high up.
OZZIE *(not looking)*. It's a Ferris wheel.

MARY. A really high Ferris wheel. We're stuck on a really high Ferris wheel. I'm stuck on a really high Ferris wheel. You may not have noticed, but I'm afraid of heights.

OZZIE. You're kidding.

MARY. No, really, I am. *(The light dawns.)* Oh, I get it, you were kidding. I'm kinda dense that way. You know, not getting it when I'm kidded.

OZZIE. You're kidding.

MARY. No, really— *(The light dawns a little quicker.)* Oh, I get it. *(She takes a look down, which increases her panic, her burbling accelerating.)* See I have this list of things I have to do, to become a successful human being. My mother wrote it for me. I have to lose ten pounds, improve my handwriting, learn Japanese, introduce myself to a stranger every day— *(Realizing her opportunity, she seizes it, extending her hand.)* Hi, I'm Mary!

OZZIE. Hi, I'm not.

MARY. —and today, my mom said I have to conquer my fear of heights. So that's why I got on the Ferris wheel. *(Another look down, more panic.)* My mom said if I can cross off every single thing on the list, I will be a better, thinner, happier, smarter, better, nicer, thinner, happier—

OZZIE. Nicer.

MARY. —person.

OZZIE *(indicating her hands, still maintaining his distant coolness).* Do you know your hands clench up into fists when you talk about the list? You look like a crazy little parakeet hanging onto its perch.

MARY *(looks down at her hands).* Wow. I mean, wow. Isn't that interesting? *(She starts shaking her hands, jiggling her fingers.)* So what about you? Why are you up here?

OZZIE. The Ferris wheel got stuck.

MARY. You are just always kidding me. *(Double take.)* You are just always kidding me, aren't you?

OZZIE. I like Ferris wheels. When you're up here, stuff down there looks small. You don't have to pay attention to any of it.

MARY. That's true. That's very true. *(Looking down.)* I can barely see my mom. Even if she yelled at me, I couldn't hear her. *(Realizing.)* And she can't hear me. *(She yells down.)* Hey, Mom, even if you yell at me to remember to stick to my low-carb diet or put on another sweater because this one makes me look fat, I can't hear you! Even if you yell at me not to bite my fingernails or laugh so loud, I can't hear you! *(She settles back.)* I like that—I like that feeling, that no one can get at me up here, not wayyyyy up here! *(Suddenly struck again with just how high up they are, she begins hyperventilating, her breath coming loudly and rapidly.)* Do you have a paper bag?

OZZIE. Not on me.

MARY. I mean, why would you. Why would anyone have a paper bag on a Ferris wheel. It's just that, if you're hyperventilating—which I am—it helps if you breathe into a paper bag. *(She gives a long, loud, wheezing breath.)*

OZZIE. Think about your right knee.

MARY. Excuse me?

OZZIE. Focus on your right knee.

MARY. Okay. *(Thinking hard.)* My right knee. My right knee. It's not my left knee, it's my right knee. Right, right, right. Knee, knee, knee. That's a very funny word if you say it enough. Knee, knee, knee. *(The light dawns.)* I get it. I'm thinking about my right knee so I can't think about being stuck on a Ferris wheel. *(Realizing—a long, loud wheeze.)* I am stuck on a Ferris wheel.

OZZIE. Think about your left knee.

MARY. I'll try, but I think the magic is gone. Maybe I could think about you telling me to think about my knee. How did you know to tell me to do that?

OZZIE. The mind can't hold two thoughts at once.

MARY. Wow. I mean, wow. That is so smart. Do you know other stuff like that?

OZZIE. I guess.

MARY. I just know the stuff I'm supposed to know. There's so much of that stuff stuck in my head, there's no room for the stuff I'd like to know. I don't even have room to think about what I'd like to know, if I had time to know anything. Which I don't. It just takes so much time to do the other stuff. You know, be a good student, good friend, good daughter—

OZZIE. A successful human being.

MARY. When I think about how mad my mom would get if I stopped doing all the things I have to do, to be all the things I have to be, I—I— *(Another wheeze.)* I really need a paper bag.

OZZIE. Think about Lincoln.

MARY. Lincoln?

OZZIE. Think about Abraham Lincoln.

MARY. Okay. *(Rapidly.)* Lincoln, Lincoln, Lincoln. *(To herself.)* What else, what else? He was tall. He got shot. He freed the slaves.

OZZIE. And everybody picked on him, all the time. Picked on what he did. What he said. How he looked. They called him ugly. They said his wife was crazy.

MARY. Wow. I mean, wow. I mean, wow that you know all that, and— *(Sadly.)* Wow, about Lincoln.

OZZIE. Everybody was at him all the time. But he went on.

MARY. Where?

OZZIE. He went on. Being. Just like he was. No matter what anyone said, they couldn't shake him.

MARY. Do you think he cried? I would have cried.

OZZIE. Maybe. But he didn't give in. I like to think about Lincoln, sitting all alone at the White House, being just how he was.

MARY. Is that what you think of, when you need to think of something else?

OZZIE *(immediately defensive—the walls going up again)*. Who says I need to do that?

MARY *(quickly)*. No one, I mean—no one. I just mean, that's how it is for me sometimes. Sometimes my brain gets so tired...

(Almost against his will, OZZIE's defenses come down again.)

OZZIE. Sometimes you just get so tired of it.

MARY. Of how you're supposed to be.

OZZIE. How you're supposed to live.

MARY. How you're supposed to look.

OZZIE. Sometimes I just wish...

MARY. Sometimes I just need...

OZZIE. Sometimes I just really need...

(BOTH react, as if to a jolt. She looks down.)

MARY. We're moving! We're going. They're letting people off. We're getting off! *(She realizes what that means.)* We're going back.

(A beat. They look at each other. OZZIE sticks out his hand.)

OZZIE. My name is Ozzie.

MARY *(helping him save face)*. Thank you, Ozzie, I mean thank you for telling me to think about my knees and talking to me. I know why you did it, to keep my mind off being scared.

OZZIE. I guess.

MARY. But if you don't mind, the next time I feel like a crazy little parakeet, and I really, really need something else to hold in my head—if you don't mind, I'm going to think about you, thinking about Lincoln.

BLACKOUT

WHAT YOU CRAVE
By Rosemary McLaughlin

CHARACTERS

MICHAEL: In his teens.

FRANKIE: Michael's older brother, also in his teens.

TIME: The present, afternoon.

PLACE: A small bedroom in a walk-up apartment near railroad tracks.

AT RISE: *MICHAEL takes out a letter and rereads it. It is addressed to his mother from their downstairs neighbors, complaining about all the noise coming from MICHAEL's apartment, from the booming stereo to the screaming family fights. Hearing FRANKIE coming up the stairs, MICHAEL puts the letter inside the envelope and slips it under the vaporizer by his bed.*

FRANKIE *(offstage)*. Maaa! Maaaa! *(Slamming doors through the apartment.)* She ain't home? *(Enters.)* Michael, she ain't home? I stay in summer school the whole day—

MICHAEL. Yeah, right.

FRANKIE. She still ain't here?

MICHAEL. Mami's working. She wants you to clean the hamster cage.

FRANKIE. Yeah. I'll clean it, then I'm gonna feed my snake hamster burgers.

MICHAEL. She says it's your turn.

FRANKIE. She says, she says. You see her here?

MICHAEL. She'll be here.

FRANKIE. Yeah, so? You gonna tell her? You gonna tell her I didn't do everything exactly like she say?
(Grabs MICHAEL playfully in a headlock.)

MICHAEL. I don't tell her nothing.

FRANKIE. You're gay.

MICHAEL. You're gay!

FRANKIE. No, you're gay!

MICHAEL. Frankie, you're gay!

FRANKIE *(smacks him on the head)*. She leave us any money?

MICHAEL. No.

FRANKIE. What I'm supposed to eat?

MICHAEL. She said we can go by Ruby's house and she'll give us hotdogs.

FRANKIE. Who?

MICHAEL. The super in 3-B. You know.

FRANKIE. You want hot dogs?

MICHAEL. No.

FRANKIE. You want pizza?

MICHAEL. Mami don't have no more credit there.

FRANKIE. Oh, man! She got to have some cash here somewheres.

MICHAEL. Yeah, you a genius, if you find that!

FRANKIE. I'm a genius when it comes to pizza! You call information for the number. 4-1-1—

MICHAEL. The phone don't work.

FRANKIE. Yeah, it do.

MICHAEL. No, it don't.

FRANKIE *(places receiver with dial tone at MICHAEL's ear)*. Mami fixed it. Dial!

MICHAEL. Where did she get the money?

FRANKIE. Paco hit the numbers. That's what they was fighting about. Don't forget the pepperoni!
(MICHAEL picks up phone; dials 911 by mistake; FRANKIE exits to rummage through other rooms.)

MICHAEL *(on phone)*. I want to order a pizza.

FRANKIE *(offstage)*. You got to ask them for the number. That's the operator.

MICHAEL *(on phone)*. No, a pizza. I need the number.

FRANKIE *(offstage)*. For the place around the corner.

MICHAEL *(on phone)*. For the place—what? No, this isn't a joke... My mother? I can't put her on the phone. *(Calling.)* Frankie! *(On phone.)* I just want to order some pizza.

FRANKIE *(off)*. What?

MICHAEL. The police are on the phone!

FRANKIE *(off)*. The police?! *(Entering.)* What!? Hang up the phone!

MICHAEL. They want to talk to someone who is in charge.

FRANKIE. Hang up the phone!

MICHAEL. My brother says I have to hang up. *(Slams phone down.)*

FRANKIE. Why are you talking to the police for?

MICHAEL. They just got on the phone. I don't know how!

FRANKIE. I told you call information!

MICHAEL. I did!

FRANKIE. What the—did you dial? Did you dial 4-1-1?

MICHAEL. Yes!

FRANKIE. No, you didn't.

MICHAEL. I did so.

FRANKIE. You didn't, mentira![1]

---

1. liar

MICHAEL. I did what you said.

FRANKIE. What did I tell you about lying to me, Michael? You lie to whoever but you don't never lie to me. Did I tell you that, Michael? Did I say that to you?

MICHAEL. I'm not lying! I did what you told me to, Frankie.

FRANKIE. Why you call the cops? You want us to get in trouble?

MICHAEL. No!

FRANKIE. You want Mami to get in trouble?

MICHAEL. No!

FRANKIE. You know what happens when she gets in trouble. You wanna go to a foster home?

MICHAEL. Don't hit me, Frankie.

FRANKIE. I ain't gonna hit you.

MICHAEL. Please don't hit me.

FRANKIE. Shut up. I ain't gonna hit you, Michael! Do I ever hit you?

MICHAEL. Yes.

FRANKIE. Cut it out. I do not... Only fooling around.

MICHAEL. Sometimes it hurts.

FRANKIE. That's 'cause you're a girl.

MICHAEL. Sometimes you make me cry.

FRANKIE. You want to cry, ninita.[2]

MICHAEL. You want to make me cry.

FRANKIE. When? When did I ever do that? You thinking about Mami. She don't stop 'til she sees you cry. She don't ever stop until she sees you cry. And once she sees you crying she be all over you saying she sorry for making you sad. Man, you got it made. You could be a ax murderer—

_____

2. baby girl

MICHAEL. I could not!

FRANKIE. You could whack Abuela, Abuelo[3]—

MICHAEL. No!!

FRANKIE. —all our cousins—

MICHAEL. I could never do that!

> *(He starts swinging at FRANKIE, who holds him back, hand to forehead.)*

FRANKIE. —and just when Mami start to whale on you, you start your blubbering and she be apologizing to you. That some racket you got. I want in on that one. That is one cool deal.

MICHAEL. How come you don't cry when Mami hits you?

FRANKIE. It's different for me.

MICHAEL. Why?

FRANKIE. It just is.

MICHAEL. Why?

FRANKIE. 'Cause I can hit her back.

MICHAEL. You would do that? You would hit her?

> *(FRANKIE moves as if to punch MICHAEL, who ducks out of the way; this is a familiar game, rough but playful; FRANKIE lifts him, wrestler-style, as if to toss him down on the floor; MICHAEL starts wheezing, FRANKIE puts him down. MICHAEL leans in toward the vaporizer to sneak another look at the letter but drops the envelope on the floor. He is having difficulty breathing.)*

FRANKIE. I want food! She don't leave us nothing?

3.Grandma, Granddad

MICHAEL. She didn't go to the store. Mami said we should go downstairs to Ruby's—maybe if we ask nice she'll make pernil...[4]

FRANKIE *(beginning to look around the room)*. I'm going out. Where does Mami keep them envelopes?

MICHAEL. I don't know.

FRANKIE. Don't she leave envelopes with cash for the rent, the numbers guy? *(Sees the envelope on the floor and picks it up.)* What's this?

MICHAEL. Yo no se.[5]

FRANKIE. Sound to me like you do. What's in here? Money?

MICHAEL. I don't know.

FRANKIE *(lightly raps MICHAEL on head)*. I told you about lying to me. What's this?

MICHAEL. I don't know.

FRANKIE. Is it a note for Mami? There's no stamp on it. Who's it from?

MICHAEL. *I don't know.*

BLACKOUT

---

4. pork roast
5. I don't know

CONVERSATION IN FOUR-PART HARMONY
By Jett Parsley

CHARACTERS

THOMAS:

MOIRA: Friends...and maybe more.

TIME: The present. Saturday afternoon.
PLACE: Thomas' home.

AT RISE: *THOMAS and MOIRA are playing Monopoly. She is also painting her toenails. He is also eating a bag of chips and drinking a Coke. She finishes paying out some money to the bank, returns to her nails.*

MOIRA. I am kickin' your butt.

THOMAS. Not for long. *(Rolls, moves.)*

MOIRA *(working on her toenails)*. Do you think Jay likes pink or red better? *(Pointing at where he landed.)* You gonna buy that? *(He looks at his money wearily.)* Good. I'll take it, then.

THOMAS. No, wait, maybe I can mortgage something. No, never mind.

MOIRA. Oh, I'll give you a break. Maybe you'll land on it later when you've won the lottery. *(Rolling, moving.)* I told you I made him apologize, right? *(THOMAS takes a drink of Coke, shoves chips in his mouth.)* Kentucky Place. Already mine. So red or pink?

THOMAS. How should I know?

MOIRA. He's your best friend. Don't you talk to your best friend?

THOMAS *(rolling, moving)*. About football. And video games.

MOIRA. And girls? Do you talk about me?

THOMAS. Jail? How many times have I been to jail in this game?

MOIRA. Kickin' your butt... *(She blows him a kiss. He rolls his eyes.)* So then he said if he'd known I'd get mad about it, he would have walked right past her.

THOMAS. These chips have, like, no salt on them. *(THOMAS needs doubles to get out of jail. He rolls a three.)* Man.

MOIRA *(rolls, moves)*. He said she didn't mean anything to him.

THOMAS *(rolls—a five)*. Oh, here, take the fifty dollars.

MOIRA. He just wants to be with me.

THOMAS *(pause)*. We don't talk about you. *(MOIRA rolls, moves her piece.)* Yes! That's mine.

MOIRA. You've got it mortgaged. You can't charge rent.

THOMAS *(rolling, moving)*. Me and Jay. We got a rule. We don't talk about the girlfriends.

MOIRA. *You* don't have a girlfriend.

THOMAS *(looking at his money)*. OK. I gotta mortgage something else. This one. Give me $200.

MOIRA *(holding the money and her toes out to him)*. Blow on my toes.

THOMAS. Not for two hundred dollars.

MOIRA. Fine. I think I'll keep most of this anyway.

THOMAS *(while she rolls)*. I got my eye on someone.

MOIRA. You do?

THOMAS *(rolling, moving)*. Community Chest. You finish that *All Quiet on the Western Front* project for Ms. Davis?

MOIRA. Yeah, I finished it.

THOMAS *(reading a card)*. Doctor's visit costs you one hundred and fifty dollars.

MOIRA. OK. So the girl you've got your eye on...

THOMAS *(counting money)*. I wanted to draw a soldier, but you know I can't draw like you can.

MOIRA. Need a loan? I'll give you one hundred and fifty dollars if you tell me who she is.

THOMAS. I've got it. *(Paying money.)* She's cute. She's fun. *(MOIRA doesn't respond.)* Think you could help me with my project?

MOIRA. Do you think Jay wasn't really sorry? Do you think he didn't just happen to bump into Liz?

THOMAS. Did I say that?

MOIRA. I could help you draw the soldier.

THOMAS. Sweet.

MOIRA *(rolls)*. I thought he was your best friend.

THOMAS *(pointing to where she lands)*. Ah-ha! That's mine. Yes, the tide will be turning now... You owe me... *(Checks his property cards.)* Twenty-two dollars.

MOIRA. Child's play. You want the soldier doing something or you just need a soldier?

THOMAS. Ms. Davis would probably like it better if he was *doing* something, like from the book, hanging out in a trench or something.

MOIRA. It's impressive how much thought you've put into this. *(About his latest move:)* There you go, boy. You owe me...with the house...

THOMAS. I don't know. Maybe I'd count *you* my best friend.

MOIRA. Really?

THOMAS. How much?

MOIRA. I'm really your best friend?

THOMAS *(looking over at her card)*. $120? Steep.

MOIRA. You're my *next* best friend.

THOMAS. After Jay.

MOIRA. Well, yeah, he's my boyfriend.

THOMAS. For a whole week. I passed Go.

MOIRA. A week is more than anyone else was giving me.

THOMAS. So you're just with him because he's there.

MOIRA. Oh, man, my polish got smudged—

THOMAS *(rolling)*. I'm just saying if the guy spends the whole night hanging out with Liz and then tells you a lie about where he was…

MOIRA. He was really sorry.

THOMAS. That's what he said. *(Moving his piece.)* Just visiting. Your turn.

MOIRA. I know what he said.

THOMAS. All right then. Your turn.

MOIRA. All right.

THOMAS *(looking at his glass)*. This Coke is flat.

(They look at the game. Pause.)

MOIRA. I think I'll go home and work on your project.

THOMAS. You know what, don't bother.

MOIRA *(pause)*. Fine. Take a D.

THOMAS *(beginning to pack up the game)*. It's not going to be a D. I'll think of something else to do with it.

MOIRA. D.

THOMAS. I'd treat you better.

MOIRA. What?

THOMAS. I sure wouldn't hook up with some girl I just bumped into at the mall.

MOIRA. He didn't actually hook up with her.

THOMAS. *I* wouldn't even *look* at her.

MOIRA *(pause)*. What are you saying?

THOMAS *(packing up the game)*. I can get on the Internet and just print out a whole bunch of pictures of soldiers.

MOIRA. D.

THOMAS. I'm not saying anything. He's my best friend. What do you think I'm saying?

MOIRA. I thought I was your best friend.

THOMAS. Man, maybe neither one of you is my best friend. Maybe you're both losers and I'm done with you.

MOIRA *(grabbing game pieces, helping him pack up)*. Give me that. I can't believe what a jerk you're being.

THOMAS. I can't believe what a *girl* you're being. "Oh, he didn't mean it. Oh, he said he was sorry."

MOIRA. Quit it, Thomas.

THOMAS. I'm out of here.

MOIRA. Don't forget your game.

THOMAS. Don't forget your nail polish.

MOIRA. Don't forget your chips.

THOMAS. Well, *do* forget my number when he breaks up with you.

MOIRA. *Do* forget my number, too.

THOMAS. Already forgot it.

MOIRA. Good!

THOMAS. Great! *(He picks up the game, heads for the door. Then he stops, turns around, comes back to her.)* One more thing I'd do different than him. I definitely wouldn't let you play games with my best friend on a Saturday afternoon when I could be with you myself— you and me, we'd be having a picnic with those jelly and marshmallow sandwiches you like and then we'd go over to the art museum and sit and stare at that painting of the woman in blue that you said you'd like to hang in your room and we'd finish it up at the baseball game and I'd buy you peanuts so you could scatter the shells in the hair of whoever sits in front of us. A guy and his girl ought to be together on a Saturday afternoon. *(Pause.)* And one more thing. I was *letting* you kick my butt. Because I know you like that. *(Pause.)*

MOIRA. Why are you saying all this?

THOMAS. Why do you think?

MOIRA. Is he with her today?

THOMAS. Does it matter?

MOIRA *(pause)*. No, I guess not. *(Pause.)* You know, the weird thing is, I never thought I ought to be with him on a Saturday afternoon. I only thought I ought to be with you. *(Pause.)* I didn't know. You felt that way.

THOMAS. Pretty rotten of me to tell you—when Jay's my best friend and all.

MOIRA. I thought *I* was your best friend.

THOMAS. Oh, yeah, well, in that case... *(She steps forward, takes his hand.)* What are you saying?

MOIRA. I'm saying I do like those jelly and marshmallow sandwiches a lot. And I do like beating your butt.

THOMAS. Don't think I'll let you do it all the time.

MOIRA. Do you like pink or red?

THOMAS. Yes.

MOIRA. Excellent. That's excellent.

BLACKOUT

PHEBE, FRIENDSHIP AND A FAT SUIT
By Claudia Haas

CHARACTERS

SHANNON: 16. Very sweet...on the surface.

HANNAH: 16. There is a wee bit of a "people pleaser" in her.

TIME: The present.

PLACE: High school—on the school steps, in the hallway or in the cafeteria.

AT RISE*: HANNAH is biting her nails. SHANNON comes rushing on—the messenger with good news.*

SHANNON. Hannah! It's up! The list is up early! *As You Like It* is cast! Mr. Frankel certainly knew what he wanted.

HANNAH. Don't tell me! I don't want to know. Did you look? Do you know? No! Don't tell me! Well... maybe...just a hint! Maybe not. Wait! No! Never mind...I need five more minutes of thinking I'm in... then maybe I'll—

SHANNON. Shut up! You're in!

HANNAH. I *said* don't tell me! *(The realization suddenly hits and HANNAH screams.)* NOOOOO!

SHANNON. Hannah!

HANNAH. Shannon!

SHANNON. I'm really happy for you, Hannah. Really, *really* happy.

HANNAH. And I'm really happy for you, Shannon. Really. Shannon? Am I happy for you?

SHANNON. Of course! Well, sort of. *(Abruptly changing.)* Don't you want to know your part?

HANNAH. Well, yeah. Of course.

SHANNON. You're Phebe. You know that mean-spirited shepherdess. The one Rosalind insults with her great monologue. You know where she talks about your inky eyes, your dark black hair...your ungrateful, wretched personality...it's great fun!

HANNAH *(not terribly sure she is thrilled with this)*. Oh. Phebe. *(Brightening up.)* Yes, it will be fun. And I made it into my first high-school play! After failing miserably the first two times. Who are you?

SHANNON. Well—I'm the understudy.

HANNAH. Oh! That's good, isn't it? I mean you get to learn all those fabulous parts. I really thought you were a shoo-in sure for Rosalind or Celia. Your audition was great.

SHANNON. Well, Mr. Frankel has been known to play favorites. And the understudy's fine—really. The understudy almost always gets in. Somewhere along the line, someone gets a failing grade or finds out theatre interferes with sports...or their social life...someone will drop, you'll see.

HANNAH. And you'll be waiting in the wings to fill in? That's great! I wonder who you will wind up being... maybe you will be Rosalind or Celia after all!

SHANNON. Maybe. So, we need to get our schedule straight. Mr. Frankel schedules lots of rehearsals—especially for Shakespeare. He will have movement workshops, dialogue workshops, makeup classes. Are you free every evening?

HANNAH. Sort of. Yes, of course. I am thinking with Phebe, I won't be called too much at the beginning. I mean, she's only in a few scenes.

SHANNON. Oh, you don't know Mr. Frankel! He wants his cast to bond. You'll be there every evening, trust me. Go home, get all your schoolwork done and be ready to camp out at the theatre for the next two months.

HANNAH. I guess I can bring my homework to rehearsal. It'll be fine.

SHANNON. Of course it will. But your homework—well, you'd better get it done during study hall. If you're not being used, you'll be working on sets and costumes.

HANNAH. I don't have a study hall. I guess, I'll just have to burn the midnight oil. Good practice for college.

SHANNON. Exactly. Get those study habits down now. You know it's interesting…

HANNAH. What?

SHANNON. Well, I heard Mr. Frankel talking and he has this really fascinating idea for the country bumpkins. You know, for you—Phebe—and Silvius and Audrey. You're going to love it!

HANNAH. Oh, tell me!

SHANNON. Well, it's not official. I mean I overheard the conversation in the hallway.

HANNAH. That's okay. I like to be prepared.

SHANNON. Well, he's going to match your character up with an animal and direct you to play the character as if it was *the* animal. Isn't that a cool concept?

HANNAH. That could be fun! I wonder what he thinks Phebe would be? Maybe, I'd be a woodland deer. Or a cute little squirrel.

SHANNON. Oh there's going to be nothing cute about Phebe. I heard Mr. Frankel state that he thinks of Phebe as a greedy little pig. Isn't that a hoot? You're going to have a pig nose and everything. It will be so funny!

HANNAH. A pig? Well, I suppose I could play her as a little pig. I guess I'd get a laugh. Not sure about the nose. I mean, is he really putting animal noses on everyone?

SHANNON. Not on everyone. I think just on you and maybe Jake and—

HANNAH. Jake? Jake Ellison? Is Jake Ellison "Silvius"?

SHANNON. Well, yeah.

HANNAH. *Jake Ellison is Silvius? I am playing opposite the coolest guy in the school????*

SHANNON. Yeah! Didn't I tell you?

HANNAH. No.

SHANNON. That is the most awesome thing about this. You're going to have a blast, Hannah.

HANNAH. Of course, I'm going to have a pig nose on...

SHANNON. And a fat suit.

HANNAH. A fat suit? What do you mean "a fat suit"?

SHANNON. Well, Mr. Frankel thinks it would be funny if Silvius went crazy worshipping this woman who is totally undesirable.

HANNAH. Undesirable. That's good for my ego.

SHANNON. In the play! You're only undesirable in the play. Besides, you never know. Mr. Frankel may change his mind.

HANNAH. Yeah. He doesn't much though, does he?

SHANNON. Change his mind? Never. But there's always a first time.

HANNAH. Still, I won't be completely hideous until dress rehearsal.

SHANNON. No. No you won't. Of course, he does like rehearsal costumes…and we already have a fat suit… and he has ordered the animal noses…

HANNAH. So, I will be hideous from day one.

SHANNON. Maybe.

HANNAH. Jake Ellison doesn't even know I'm alive. Now, he'll only picture me as an oinking, snouted, chubby little slovenly sow.

SHANNON. It's not that bad. I mean, it's for the good of the play.

HANNAH. So, I'm going to be a pig in front of the whole student body.

SHANNON. Well, at least no one will recognize you. Especially with the wig.

HANNAH. The wig?

SHANNON. Yeah, you know the wig that has the bald spot in the front and then these little gray hairs that go everywhere?

HANNAH. Didn't John wear that as Scrooge in *A Christmas Carol*?

SHANNON. That's the one!

HANNAH. Why would a pig wear Scrooge's wig?

SHANNON. Because it would be funny, don't you think?

HANNAH. I suppose. Gee, I wonder what they'll do to Jake. It'll be hard to make him look funny.

SHANNON. Oh, no! They're going to make him super cute. Maybe a deer nose or something like that? See, it will be funnier if someone super cute goes off crying for love for someone…let's just say not so cute. Really not cute. In fact, horrible. A fright. An eyesore. Really, *really...*

HANNAH. Ugly.

SHANNON. Now, I didn't say "ugly"! Unsightly. Yeah, that's a better description.

HANNAH. Unsightly. No wonder I got cast.

SHANNON. Don't take it personally. I'm talking about the character, not you. Besides, it's an honor to be in a play. Especially a Shakespearean one.

HANNAH. Yeah, well, "what I did for love" and all that stuff, right?

SHANNON. Right.

HANNAH. Well, I guess I should move on home and get some work done...do you think it's possible that Mr. Frankel might change his mind about some of that stuff? You know, make me look, well—not quite so... unsightly?

SHANNON. Sure, it's possible.

HANNAH. But not very probable.

SHANNON. I'm almost afraid to tell you the other stuff.

HANNAH. There's more?

SHANNON. Well, sort of...but you never know. It might not happen. We'll wait and see.

HANNAH. What? *What?*

SHANNON. Well, I don't want to upset you...

HANNAH. Shannon! You can just drop something and let it stay in the air like that? It's like there's a little gremlin following me around chanting "There's more! There's more!"

SHANNON. All right. But promise me you won't get upset. I mean, none of this may come true.

HANNAH. I won't...get...*upset!*

SHANNON. Well, Mr. Frankel sort of mentioned that he *might* add some snorting to your lines.

HANNAH. Whaaaaaat?

SHANNON. Just a little. You do snort, don't you?

HANNAH. *Snort?* What do you mean, do I snort? *Who snorts?*

SHANNON. Well, you know Shakespeare went for some pretty low humor. He's going to pull out all the stops with your character. He has you snorting all over the place. Really gross. The audience will love it!

HANNAH. I need to talk to Mr. Frankel!

SHANNON. I wouldn't do that right now. He's in conference with Mr. Salzburg the set designer. When they get going, things are intense. They're not fond of interruptions.

HANNAH. Listen, Shannon. I can wear a pig nose. So, they give me a snout—fine! I can live with that. You want to change my physical appearance? Well, I guess that's what actors do for their character. The fat suit does not thrill me but you know—all for the good of the play. Fine. It's fine. If they want me to be a pig wearing Scrooge's wig to get a laugh, I can do that. I'm easy. But no way, no how, am I going to snort through a play. I do not snort Shakespeare! I did not snort at my audition and I will not snort in front of the entire student body! Snorting is the final straw! I'm going home now. And I am not coming back for first reading. You can tell Mr. Frankel that I decline the role of "Snorting Snout Face"! I'm out of here. *(HANNAH exits.)*

SHANNON *(smiling).* Score one for the understudy.

BLACKOUT

GRILLED CHEESE

By Doug Cooney

CHARACTERS

MANDY: 14. Impetuous. Has put herself on a bus to visit her grandmother in a convalescent home.
STAR: A teenage runaway.
BENNY: A teenage runaway.

TIME: The present.
PLACE: A bus station.

AT RISE: *SFX: Public announcements, engines rev, hydraulic hiss. MANDY on her cell phone. STAR appears. A homeless girl.*

MANDY. Dad? Are you there, Dad? Pick up, Dad. Grrrr. Dad, I'm in the middle of a bus station in Rockford, Illinois, and you're never around when I need you so I'm leaving this message on your voice mail to let you know that— *(A loud, triple beep.)* Oh, no! Battery dead. Stupid cell phone.
STAR. You could sell that phone, you know.
MANDY. Sell it? Or I could just recharge the battery. Hello?
STAR. I know where you could sell it if you wanted to. Just so you know.
MANDY. Why would I sell it?
STAR. Make some easy cash. Everybody needs money.

MANDY. I already have money.

STAR. You got money?

MANDY. Yes. So I don't think I need to—

STAR. Great. So. Whatever you got will help. Thanks.

MANDY. I'm sorry?

STAR. You gonna help me or what?

MANDY. Help you with what?

STAR. Money.

MANDY. I'm not giving you my money.

STAR. Hey. I'd help you.

(BENNY appears. A homeless boy.)

BENNY. Hey, Star.

STAR. Benny.

BENNY. You ask already?

STAR *(lies)*. I asked. She doesn't have any money.

BENNY. She's got money.

STAR. I asked and she said no. *(To MANDY.)* You don't have any money. No money, right?

MANDY *(wary, but playing along)*. No. I'm broke.

STAR. Told you so. Let's get outta here.

BENNY. Hold up, hold up. She looks hungry to me. You hungry?

MANDY. I got some crackers from some guy on the bus.

BENNY. Crackers? I'm talking better than crackers. Star here makes a fine grilled cheese sandwich.

STAR. Oh, yeah. Thank you. Hold the applause.

BENNY. She puts the cheese between bread, wraps some foil—then we wait for a truck off the highway, one that's coming from really far—

STAR. So the engine is real hot.

BENNY. Slap our sandwiches on the hood. Few minutes. Presto! Grilled cheese sandwich. Just like home.

STAR. The secret is the cheese.

BENNY. Let's rustle up some cheese! Fix you right up.

MANDY. I don't want a grilled cheese fresh off some bumper.

BENNY. You'll be saying—this is as good as Mom's!

STAR. Thank you. Thank you. Hold the applause.

MANDY. If I wanted a grilled cheese like Mom's, I think I'd just go home to Mom. Okay?

STAR. Where'd you run from? Benny ran away from Houston.

BENNY. And Star ran from Detroit. We got the whole Houston-Detroit connection.

STAR. We watch each other's back.

BENNY. We're tight.

STAR. Only not like boyfriend/girlfriend.

BENNY. No. Not like that.

STAR. Like brother and sister.

BENNY. Brother and sister. That's all right.

STAR. Family.

BENNY. Like that.

MANDY. Excuse me. You think I'm a runaway. I am not a runaway. Do I look like a runaway to you?

BENNY & STAR. Yeah.

BENNY. We're not "runaways." We call ourselves "freedom fighters"! We're headed for New York City. You ever been to New York?

MANDY. New York? I would kill to go to New York.

BENNY. That's where we're going.

STAR. Where you going?

MANDY. Here. I'm not a runaway. I'm just moving from my mom's to my…

BENNY. You're moving here? Do you know where you are? There's nothing here! This place is nowhere!

STAR. It's okay but it's not that hot.

BENNY. You should come. Star and me know the road. We know how to travel. Meet people, take in the sights, check out the view. A few laughs, a couple adventures. Rustle up a grilled cheese if we get hungry. And every day, New York City gets closer on the horizon.

MANDY. I've always wanted to see New York.

BENNY. Here's your chance.

MANDY. Oh, I could never. I got my grandmother—

BENNY. Sure you could.

STAR. Benny, she's not interested.

BENNY. Sure, she's interested. The only thing is—it's gonna cost money to get to New York.

STAR. She doesn't have any money, Benny. I told you.

MANDY. Right. No money.

BENNY. No money? Not even anything to sell?

MANDY. I better be going. I really have to get to—

BENNY. That's a nice jacket.

MANDY. My mom got it for me.

BENNY. Looks expensive. Bet it cost a lot of money.

MANDY. It's foreign. I think it's Italian.

BENNY. You could get a lot of money for that jacket.

MANDY. I'm not selling my jacket. What is it with you two? You're trying to sell my jacket, she's trying to sell my cell phone—

BENNY. You got a cell phone? Star didn't say nothing about a cell phone.

STAR. It's busted, Benny.

BENNY. Busted? Lemme see.

MANDY. It's not busted. It's just got a dead battery.

BENNY. You can still sell it with a dead battery.

MANDY. It's not for sale! What is it with you guys?

BENNY. How you gonna get to New York if it's not for sale? You gotta have something for sale. Pretty little rich girl. Wearing your nice clothes and—such pretty hair. Doesn't she have pretty hair, Star?

STAR. Yeah, she's got pretty hair.

BENNY. Can I touch your pretty hair?

MANDY. I'm late. I gotta get outta here.

BENNY *(grabbing MANDY)*. What's your hurry?

MANDY. I'm headed to Grandma's. A cab and I'm there. I could walk!

STAR. Let her go, Benny. She's not made for the road like we are.

BENNY. You got a soft touch, Star. You're not made for the road with a soft touch like that.

STAR. Let her go! I'll scream, Benny. I'll call a cop.

BENNY. You wouldn't call a cop on me.

STAR. I have before.

BENNY. You keep saying that, but you never have.

STAR. Help! Help! Somebody help! Police! Police! *(BENNY runs off.)*

MANDY. You didn't have to do that for me.

STAR. Sure I did. You're in more trouble than you think.

MANDY. I'm not in trouble. My dad's gonna pick me up as soon as I call him.

STAR. A minute ago, it was your grandma.

MANDY. My dad or my grandma. Look. I'm just sitting here. It's not like I'm a runaway.

STAR. I see a sister, sitting by herself, cell phone don't work, clutching her knapsack and her nice little jacket—a girl in a bus station running through her options and thinking out loud—talking to strangers—a girl like that is learning to live by her wits. You may not think you're a runaway but you're running from something.

MANDY. It's not like that.

STAR. However, whatever. We're not so different, you and me.

MANDY. Are you in trouble with Benny now?

STAR. Not likely. He gets hungry. I'll make a grilled cheese sandwich and he'll cool down. We fight but he watches my back. I cook. We watch after each other. It's like that. I know you think it's gross, but my grilled cheese is better than you think. Thank you, thank you, hold the applause.

MANDY *(searches for change)*. Hold up. I got some money if you need it.

STAR. Keep your change. There's a pay phone by the ladies'.

MANDY. But don't you need money?

STAR. Not your money.

MANDY. Hold up. Crackers?

STAR. Girl, keep your crackers. You're gonna need them more than you think.

BLACKOUT

THE PURPOSE OF A KITCHEN
By Tammy Ryan

CHARACTERS

MORGAN: 17. About to start her senior year in high school. Idealistic, yet naive. Thinks of herself as an activist, yet is unsure of the path she should take after graduation.

CAROL: 46. Morgan's mother. A suburban stay-at-home mom about to face an empty nest. She wants the best for Morgan, yet feels that while it all seems to be starting for Morgan, it is basically over for herself.

TIME: The present.
PLACE: The kitchen. Morning.

AT RISE: *MORGAN enters and sees CAROL asleep in a comfy chair pulled up to the kitchen table. The computer is still on. MORGAN begins banging around making coffee. CAROL wakes up, checks the computer screen and is about to shut it off.*

MORGAN. Don't shut down! I want to check my mail.
CAROL. I didn't hear you come in last night.
MORGAN. I didn't.
CAROL. What do you mean, you didn't?
MORGAN. It got late so I spent the night at Kristen's.
CAROL. You need to call when you do that.

MORGAN. I did call...the line was busy. One more reason to get another phone line.

CAROL. Forget it.

MORGAN. Okay, but if we had another phone line or voice mail like the rest of the civilized world, I could've left a message. Excuse me. *(She signs onto the computer.)*

CAROL. A better use of your time would be to start those essays for your college applications—

MORGAN. I know, I know, I am working on them, subconsciously, okay, every second that I breathe I am contemplating my "goals and dreams" for the future, *or* "where I see myself in five years" while I do other things more pressing at the moment.

CAROL. Like e-mail.

MORGAN. You don't believe in voice mail, all I'm left with is e-mail.

CAROL. How was your meeting?

MORGAN. You don't care.

CAROL. I just asked you, didn't I?

MORGAN. You "care" in that you "care" about me, but as far as what the meeting was about, you don't care.

CAROL. It was something political, right?

MORGAN. That's right, Mom.

CAROL. Well in between your political activities you better get started on those applications, because early admissions increases your chances of getting into the school you want.

MORGAN. Mom, did you sign that forward I sent you?

CAROL. What forward?

MORGAN. The forward calling for an end to the inhumane treatment of women in Afghanistan?

CAROL. No, I didn't sign it.

MORGAN. Did you forward it back to me then?

CAROL. Oh, I don't know.

MORGAN. I don't have it in my mailbox.

CAROL. Then I guess I didn't.

MORGAN. Did you save it?

CAROL. I guess I deleted it.

MORGAN. What??

CAROL. Morgan, I don't have time for those endless e-mails you're always sending me.

MORGAN. And you claim to be interested in what I'm doing? I bet you didn't even read it.

CAROL. I read it.

MORGAN. And? *(Beat.)* Are you not horrified by what's happening to those women? They can't go to school, they can't receive medical treatment, they can't feed their children, because they can't work or even beg in the streets. They are being systematically killed if they don't stay hidden in their houses. A woman driving down the street was pulled from her car and stoned to death by a group of men because her arm was showing.

CAROL *(overlapping)*. I read it, Morgan. What can I say, I feel sorry for those women.

MORGAN. It's not just about women. They blew up the Bamiyan Buddahs and you don't even care.

CAROL. I don't even know what they are.

MORGAN. They are just giant religious icons for an entire culture. Women and Art. That's what they hate. And that's just the beginning, they'll be after everybody sooner or later, while people like you sit and watch it on TV.

CAROL. When did this happen?

MORGAN. Years ago, Mom. They blew them up in March 2001, which you would know if you ever read your mail. I sent you an e-mail when it happened. You must have deleted that too.

CAROL. I don't see how signing an e-mail is going to change anything.

MORGAN. No you wouldn't. You're a Wal-Mart shopper.

CAROL. What is that supposed to mean?

MORGAN. It means you don't care about the truth behind things.

CAROL. I like shopping at Wal-Mart. They have low prices. I don't care if they are politically inconvenient—

MORGAN. Try morally bankrupt—

CAROL. It's cheap, that's why I shop there. And that's why everybody else does too.

MORGAN. What's cheap to you are these women's lives. You couldn't even lift a finger.

CAROL. I did lift a finger; I deleted it.

MORGAN. All the names on that petition are now lost, I specifically said to send it back to me if you weren't—

CAROL. Oh come on, everyone deletes those things.

MORGAN. I *don't*. My friends don't. The people I communicate with all over the world don't.

CAROL. Even if it *got* to someone who could do something about it, they would delete it because they don't care either.

MORGAN. They should.

CAROL. Of course they should, but they don't, that's reality.

MORGAN. And you know all about reality.

CAROL. What am I supposed to do, Morgan? Go to Afghanistan and personally wage war against all the stone-throwing icon-destroying men? I could go to Iran and Iraq while I'm at it; why not the Philippines and Guatemala and everywhere else life is hard for women, forget that I have my own life to live.

MORGAN. Yeah. Renovating your kitchen for the hundredth time.

CAROL. Have I redone this kitchen ninety-nine times?

MORGAN *(turns away from computer to face CAROL. Calmly)*. What is the purpose of a kitchen?

CAROL. The purpose? To cook food.

MORGAN. But you never cook.

CAROL. I cooked last night.

MORGAN. Once in a hundred years.

CAROL. We are in the midst of renovations so I *can cook every night*, that's the point.

MORGAN. There is no point to your life, Mom: that's the point.

CAROL *(drinking her coffee, weary)*. It's an ordinary life, Morgan.

MORGAN. There is a whole world of people out there, *(gesturing toward computer)* that for them, the way we live is shameful.

CAROL. Because I want an updated kitchen?

MORGAN. The way we *waste*. The way we *consume. shopping* for cheap crap at *Wal-Mart*, while little brown people die working in factories for pennies so we can redo a perfectly good kitchen that we don't even use because—

CAROL. I need more cabinet space!

MORGAN. But it never satisfies, Mom, that's why you have to keep doing it. The only thing that satisfies is helping other people, but you have no idea about that because your life is so small.

CAROL. Excuse me. I help people. I help you. I help your father and your grandparents and I help the neighbors, sometimes.

MORGAN. That's good, but our responsibilities don't end there.

CAROL. My job is not to right every wrong in the world.

MORGAN. Then what is your job?

CAROL. I quit my job seventeen years ago so I could take care of my family, and make us all happy.

MORGAN. Happiness is your job?

CAROL. Yes, why not?

MORGAN. That is the most selfish thing I've heard in my life. It's time for a new job, Mom.

CAROL. Why? That's what you're doing. All your politics, you do for yourself.

MORGAN. Excuse me, I have to take a shower, then I'm going back to Kristen's where we will be writing letters to save a woman's *life*, while you pick out little knobs for your cabinets.

BLACKOUT

DON'T TELL
By Kristina M. Schramm

CHARACTERS

ODA MAE DAVIS: 20. Heavyset black woman who is mentally challenged.

EDINA MELKAMPF: 12. Precocious.

TIME: The present. Oda Mae lives a stable, but isolated life with her parents in a quiet suburb. When lonely Edina Melkampf moves in next door, the two become fast friends. Edina's past is shrouded in mystery and she lives in a self-created fantasy world based on her favorite book, *Peter Pan*. Oda Mae has her own fantasy. She wants to have a wedding. The friends divide their time between acting out scenes from *Peter Pan* and planning an elaborate wedding. Eventually Oda Mae's parents agree to throw a "mock wedding" for their daughter. Edina plays the part of the groom.

PLACE: The scene takes place after most of the wedding guests have gone home. In the darkness of Oda Mae's bedroom, still dressed in wedding attire, they talk about the previous evening, when Edina's fragile fantasy world collided with reality.

AT RISE: *After several moments, ODA MAE breaks the silence.*

ODA MAE. Why are you sitting in the dark?

EDINA. I got a headache.

ODA MAE. You ain't got no headache. You been cryin' again. *(EDINA shakes her head.)* I can see you have.

EDINA. Is everybody gone? *(ODA MAE shakes her head.)* Why can't everybody just go home?

ODA MAE. I can't exactly ask them to leave. It's my wedding after all.

EDINA. It's not like it's a *real* wedding.

ODA MAE. Everybody brought me presents. That's real enough for me.

EDINA. It's still just pretend.

ODA MAE. "Nothing *pretend* about feeding all them people." That's what my daddy said.

EDINA. It's a game, Oda Mae…just like when we play *Peter Pan.*

ODA MAE. This ain't nothing like *Peter Pan.* When we play that you only let me be Wendy and she never wear anything but that old nightgown. Now if…

EDINA. That's not what I…

ODA MAE. …you'd ever let me be Tinkerbell—like I'm always asking to—I could've wore a beautiful fairy costume. But, no. I always got to be Wendy. Well, look at me now. Have you ever seen anything so pretty? Don't you think I look pretty?

EDINA. I guess…

ODA MAE. You guess? That the best you can do?

EDINA. How can you think about your dress at a time like this! Don't you know we have bigger problems?

ODA MAE. We got problems all right. The ceremony ain't been over but a couple of hours and we already having our first argument.

EDINA. We're not married! *(Gestures to her own tuxedo shirt and pants.)* This is just a costume!

ODA MAE. I know! I'm slow, not stupid. I was just teasing. Why'd you have to go and spoil everything? Can't I have a little fun after all I been through?

EDINA. What about me? What about what I've been through! I'm the one...

ODA MAE. Hush! Don't even start. I don't want to talk about you right now. I don't want to talk at all. Just let me go to bed. I'm near too tired to move. Every bone in my body aches. Oh! *(Suddenly puts her hand to her chest.)* That's a whole new pain.

EDINA. Are you okay? Should I get your mother?

ODA MAE. It's probably just indigestion.

EDINA. Are you sure it's not your condition?

ODA MAE. My what?

EDINA. You know. *(Pause.)* Your *heart* condition.

ODA MAE. Girl, where do you come up with this stuff?

EDINA. You don't have a heart condition? Then what is wrong with you?

ODA MAE. I got asthma.

EDINA. That's it?

ODA MAE. It ain't enough? You sound like you sorry I ain't got nothing more serious wrong with me. Asthma can kill you, you know!

EDINA. Sorry! Don't be so sensitive.

ODA MAE. Sensitive? Me? How can you say that? After last night...

EDINA. I said I was sorry.

ODA MAE. Besides, if I did have a heart condition, we wouldn't be having this conversation because I would've dropped down dead from all that digging.

EDINA. I thought you didn't want to talk about it.

ODA MAE. You the one started. And just 'cause I been all happy and smiling with them folks today doesn't mean I forgot what happened yesterday. I told you I ain't stupid.

EDINA. I never said you were.

ODA MAE. I couldn't even enjoy my own wedding cake...chocolate with cinnamon frosting...my favorite! And now, when I finally stop thinking about last night for one minute, you go and bring it up again.

EDINA. Sorry.

ODA MAE. Sorry don't keep me from seeing that hole in the ground...

EDINA. Stop...

ODA MAE. and those eyes...

EDINA. Stop...

ODA MAE. looking up at me like he was still alive! Lord have mercy!

EDINA. Oda Mae! Don't!

ODA MAE. Edina, what if he ain't dead? What if he's digging his way out with one of your own shovels this very minute?

EDINA. He's dead, Oda Mae! He's dead!

ODA MAE. But what if he's not *all the way* dead. What if he comes to get you...and Oda Mae?

EDINA. I told you he's...

ODA MAE. I wish you'd never told me nothing.

EDINA. You wanted to help!

ODA MAE. Hang the wash! You never said anything about burying no pirate. Look at my hands! What if this rash gets worse? What am I going to tell my momma?

EDINA. It's probably from lime.

ODA MAE. Lime? Why you got lime in the basement in the first place?

EDINA. My mom uses it in the garden.

ODA MAE. Does it give her a rash?

EDINA. She wears gloves.

ODA MAE. Now you tell me!

EDINA. Look, I didn't even know it was there. It must have been with all those bags of dirt. *(Beat.)* Oh, Oda Mae! What if my mom notices all those bags of dirt are missing?

ODA MAE. Girl, what if she notices you got a body in your basement? *(Beat.)* Edina, I been thinking. Maybe you'd be better off telling your momma the whole thing, soon as she gets back.

EDINA. What?

ODA MAE. Just tell her the truth and...

EDINA. You want me to tell her I murdered somebody?

ODA MAE. You didn't murder nobody. It was an accident.

EDINA. She won't believe me.

ODA MAE. Sure she will. I do. I could tell her what happened and *(beat)* when the police come, I could tell them, too!

EDINA. The police? Now you're going to tell the police? Oda Mae, do you *want* me to go to jail?

ODA MAE. You won't go to jail when I tell them it was an accident.

EDINA. They won't believe you! They never believe anybody! Don't you watch television? The police ask a guy a couple of questions and before the first commercial he's in jail.

ODA MAE. But if you tell the truth...

EDINA. The truth? "Captain Hook was in my basement and I killed him!" Is that what you want me to tell them?

ODA MAE *(beat)*. Edina, are you sure it was him? *(EDINA nods.)* Maybe it was just a bum looking for a handout... *(EDINA shakes her head.)* ...or trying to steal something? Ever think of that?

EDINA. You think I'm making it up?

ODA MAE. I'm just saying, in the book Captain Hook had long dark hair and a patch over...

EDINA. That's a fairy tale, Oda Mae! This is real! In real life pirates don't wear patches. They disguise themselves so you can never tell who they are. They look like...anybody.

ODA MAE. Anybody?

EDINA. ...even someone you'd never think, someone you trust...

ODA MAE. You trying to scare Oda Mae?

EDINA. No, it's the truth!

ODA MAE. But if he was wearing a disguise, how did you know it was Hook?

EDINA. Because...because...I've seen him before...

ODA MAE. You have?

EDINA. When I was little...he used to come to our house when I was alone.

ODA MAE. You never told me! I thought I was your best friend.

EDINA. I didn't remember until last night. Before that I thought...I don't know what I thought. My mom said...

ODA MAE. You told your momma about Hook?

EDINA. When I told her about how he disguised himself...how he used to come in and lock me up...she didn't believe me. She said I spent too much time reading stories...that I was confused, imagining things.

ODA MAE. Well, you can tell me. I'll believe you.

EDINA. No you won't. Nobody ever believes me.

ODA MAE. I will.

EDINA. Really? *(ODA MAE nods vigorously.)* And if I tell you, you promise, you won't tell anybody anything?

ODA MAE. I promise.

EDINA. Not even your momma?

ODA MAE. I said I promise.

EDINA. Cross your heart and hope to die?

ODA MAE. I'll cross anything you want, Edina, just tell me what he looked like.

EDINA. My dad. He looked like my dad.

BLACKOUT

HOPELESS
By Julia Rose

Hopeless was first performed in 2003 by the Beth Jacob Congregation Youth Group in Mendota Heights, Minnesota. It was directed by JoAnn Pasternack and featured Anna Allen, Leora Allen and Talia Minsberg.

CHARACTERS

MAYA: Drama queen.
RACHEL: Peacemaker.
AMY: Self-centered.

TIME: The present.
PLACE: A slumber party.

AT RISE: *The slumber party is in high gear.*

MAYA. I'll never get over this!
RACHEL. What are you talking about?
AMY. You'll be fine!
MAYA. No I won't! I'm just going to die!
RACHEL. You're not going to die.
MAYA. Yes I am. I just can't live without him!
RACHEL. You were only going out for three weeks!
MAYA. Well it was the best three weeks of my life.
AMY. He's not that great.
MAYA. He's amazing.
RACHEL. He's a jerk.

MAYA. He's nice, and he's funny, and he's in AP math, and I can't believe he dumped me!

(MAYA bursts into tears. AMY and RACHEL give each other looks.)

RACHEL. We have to get her mind off of him!

(Phone rings. MAYA runs to the phone. AMY and RACHEL start looking through a magazine.)

MAYA. Hello? Oh...hi...yeah...I'm fine, I'll call you later. Bye.

RACHEL. Did you really think that he would call?

AMY. This is going to be a long night.

RACHEL. Amy!

AMY. Here, there's a quiz, "Will You Ever Date Again?" *(MAYA starts crying)* Okay, let's find a different one. Here, "How You Know When You Are Over Your Man."

RACHEL. Perfect.

AMY. Question One: The last time you thought about your ex was A. A few days ago, B. You can't even remember, or C. The last time? You never stopped thinking about him?

MAYA. C. I never stopped thinking about him.

RACHEL. Maybe it's too soon for this quiz.

AMY. Question Two: You spot the hottie you used to date at the mall. He's with another girl, and you are with your mom. What do you do? A. Check your reflection in your compact and calmly continue walking, B. Run up to the new girl and start telling her what a bad kisser he is, or C. Run away?

MAYA. How could he already be with a new girl? It's only been a few hours.

AMY. I would say C.

RACHEL. Okay, Question Three: The school winter dance is approaching and so far you have no date. You A. Aren't worried because you are so sure that your ex will ask you, B. Ask a random guy on the street, or C. go with a friend?

MAYA. Oh who cares! I never want to be seen in public again! I'm just going to lie on this bed and die.

AMY. Oh, give me the magazine! Question Four: When your boyfriend breaks up with you, you drive your friends A. Crazy, B. Totally insane, C. Positively psycho, D. Incredibly delirious, or E. All of the above?

RACHEL. You're horrible! We're here to help, not make her cry.

(Phone rings. MAYA lunges for it.)

MAYA. Hello? Hi Dad. Yes, everything is fine. Rachel and Amy are here. Okay. I love you, too. Bye.

RACHEL. He's really not going to call.

MAYA. Maybe he will, you don't know.

AMY. Okay. Let's see what this quiz says about you... you are nine to twelve points, "Hopelessly Still in Love."

RACHEL. Great.

AMY. "Get over him, girlfriend! He's moving on and you should, too. Buy a new pair of shoes, go clubbing, or eat some ice cream with your friends, but just get over him! He's not the guy for you."

(MAYA starts crying again.)

RACHEL. I'm not sure that was such a good idea.

AMY. I'm going to go make some popcorn.

MAYA. Isn't that fattening?

AMY. Don't worry, it's the ninety-four percent fat free kind. *(AMY exits.)*

RACHEL. Do you want a makeover?

MAYA. I guess. I'm so depressed that I don't really care what I look like.

RACHEL. Why do you care so much about him? I mean, he dumped you at a school dance. That's pretty jerky.

MAYA. It's just that we had such an amazing connection. Do you know what it feels like to have someone to talk to every night about what you ate for lunch that day or what you just saw on TV?

RACHEL. No, and I don't really think that I want to.

MAYA. It was just nice knowing that someone cared.

RACHEL. I care about you.

MAYA. I know.

RACHEL. Seriously. I do.

MAYA. Thanks.

RACHEL. And Amy does, too.

MAYA. Sometimes I'm not so sure.

RACHEL. She does. Just sometimes it's hard for her to act like it.

MAYA. Okay. *(Disbelieving.)*

RACHEL. Like you know how when boys have a crush on you they act like the biggest jerks ever?

MAYA. Are you saying that Amy has a crush on me?

RACHEL. No.

MAYA. So what then?

RACHEL. I guess, I think that she's kinda jealous of you.

MAYA. Seriously?

RACHEL. Yeah. I mean, you had a boyfriend, and she never did, and you have kissed a boy, and she never has—

MAYA. Well…

RACHEL. You guys never kissed?

MAYA. It was never the right situation.

RACHEL. Well, Amy at least thinks that you guys kissed. And she always thought that she would be the first one of us to date and stuff.

MAYA. I guess you're right.

RACHEL. And besides, don't worry about Mike. My older sister always says that junior-high dating is so pointless. Maybe she's right.

MAYA. Yeah, she did teach us how to curl our eyelashes.

RACHEL. So don't freak out. You'll find someone else, to talk about food with, or whatever.

MAYA. I guess. I mean, I wasn't going to marry him anyways.

RACHEL. Of course not. Think what your kids would look like!

MAYA. He does have really nice eyes.

RACHEL. But his nose!

(They both laugh.)

MAYA. Do you want to hear a secret?

RACHEL. Yes!

MAYA. I kinda have a crush on someone else!

RACHEL. For real? Who?

MAYA. Kevin.

RACHEL. No way!

MAYA. Yeah. And he was totally flirting with me tonight, don't you think?

RACHEL. Yeah, sure.

(AMY enters with a bowl of popcorn.)

AMY. Oh my gosh, guys, I totally forgot to tell you what happened to me tonight!

MAYA. What?

AMY. I had my first kiss!

RACHEL. What?

MAYA. How could you forget to tell us something like that?

AMY. Well, I was trying to pay attention to you. You take up a lot of time.

MAYA. Hey!

RACHEL. Who'd you kiss?

AMY. Kevin. *(MAYA starts to cry.)* Oh no, what's wrong?

RACHEL. Maya thought that he liked her.

AMY. Why would she think that?

(MAYA cries louder. RACHEL gives AMY a look.)

RACHEL. Maya, it's okay. It's probably too soon for you to move on anyways.

AMY. Definitely.

MAYA. You're right. So how was it? Was it nice?

AMY. Kind of. I mean, it was really quick and kind of slobbery. I'm sure that you and Mike had better kisses. *(MAYA looks away.)* Right, Maya? *(Pause.)* You don't have to be shy, you can tell us. *(Pause.)* You did kiss him, didn't you, Maya?

RACHEL. Maybe we should talk about something else.

MAYA. Well, I mean…

AMY. Oh my gosh! Three weeks?

RACHEL. Amy!

(Phone rings.)

MAYA. Hello? Oh, hi Kevin. Sure. Amy, it's Kevin. He wants to talk to you.

AMY. Really? *(RACHEL gives AMY a look.)* I mean, fine. Hello? Yeah. Thank you. Really? Okay? Really? Okay. Really? Yeah, I'll be there. Okay. Great. Really? Okay. Bye. Oh my gosh, Kevin and I just had the greatest conversation!

RACHEL. It sounded wonderful.

AMY. It was! And he asked me out on a date!

MAYA. Really?

AMY. Well, kind of. He asked me if I would be at soccer practice tomorrow.

RACHEL. That's not a date.

AMY. Well, it kind of is.

(MAYA starts crying.)

RACHEL. There she goes again.

(Phone rings.)

MAYA. Will someone else get it? I'm too depressed.

(RACHEL and AMY look at each other.)

RACHEL. Hello? Hi Mike. Yeah, she's right here.

MAYA. Hello? Hi. Yeah. Really? Me too. Oh yeah, it was fun… *(MAYA improvs talking on the phone.)*

AMY. Soccer practice isn't really a date, is it?

RACHEL. No.

AMY. We are such losers.

RACHEL. Yeah.

AMY. Should we take the quiz?

RACHEL. Sure.

AMY. "Will You Ever Date Again? Question One: What did you do last Saturday night? A. Sat at home in sweatpants, B. Partied all night, or, C. Hung out with friends?

RACHEL. A.

AMY. Me too.

RACHEL. We're hopeless.

MAYA *(still talking on phone)*. Oh, that sounds like so much fun! Yeah! Definitely! Okay!…

BLACKOUT

CLASSROOM MONOLOGUES

A ROSE IS A ROSE
By David Alex

(ANGELA, 16, has been arguing with her mother. She surprises herself when she finds a way to "make a deal" and communicate with her mother. ANGELA has a rose tattoo and several piercings.)

Angela

Chill out—it's not your body. And since this is my rose—I paid for it with my money—you got nothing to say... You don't like this—fine, don't look at it. You don't like the clothes on my floor—fine, shut the door. And if you don't like me, don't look at me either. My friends—I couldn't care less what you think about them. At least they're not phony like yours.

That Shirley woman—the one you play golf with—oh, please. As two-sided as they come. Why, if her husband didn't work for Dad, she wouldn't give us the time o' day. As it is, she can hardly tell time without a digital watch. And Beverly; whatever. She's so tanked up, all she needs to do is breathe in the gas tank and her car'll go forever.

At least my friends are real—and can stand up at the end of the day. So don't even think about talkin' about my generation. When you were my age, all your generation cared about was going up in space. Well, I'm into space too. My space. And right now, you're in it... Listen, just listen. Before you start yellin' again, remember that at smokin' dope and sleepin' around with everyone like you guys did way back in the '60s. Free love—what a joke. For me, love will be something special... Right. Like some guy's gonna fall in love with me and then dump me 'cause of a rose. No way. Or like Dad would leave you if you came home with one too? *(Laughs.)* Show Dad we've both got minds of our own. C'mon. It doesn't have to be a rose. I mean, I'm into roses, you know that. You—you're not a rose kind. Too—flowery. You're more of a...of a—oh, yeah, I got it. This is too much. Listen to this. Ruby slippers... For a Judy Garland freak like you—it's perfect. Two slippers, the heels almost touching. It'd be like—okay, here it is. When you walk or stand up, it'd be like two heels clicking!

(She makes a clicking noise.)

Perfect. You get the tattoo, and I'll make you a deal—three deals for your one... I'll leave the door of my room closed while the floor is covered with my clothes. You won't see a thing.

(Indicating her ear, nose or lip.)

Second, no more than three new holes—and that includes the tongue and bellybutton. And—oh, you'll love this. We'll do lunch—in the mall. And afterwards, I'll give you a hug in front of all your friends... 'Course, if any of mine are around, forget it. Let's not go extreme here. Whataya say, Mom, ya ready to get a life?

(She clicks her heels.)

PIRATE GIRL
By Ric Averill

(MAGGIE is gathered with a group of other young women. One of the girls asks her if dressing distinctively is a statement or a form of showing off. MAGGIE smiles and says it's Johnny's fault.)

Maggie

I told him I was a pirate.

He stared at me every day. I'd been wearing scarves for a long time. When I was little, I wore them because I liked them. My Aunt Jean collected them, Mom always knew what to get for Aunt Jean's birthday. She always had on a different scarf—every time I saw her. She was a realtor and Mom said she always "had to look her best" 'cause she was always "showing."

I thought "showing" was a bad thing, you know, when it's your slip or strap—but I guess it works pretty well for a businesswoman like Jean. When I hit seventh grade, my scarves started finding their way to different places. It was just what I did. Some were so long I could wear them around my waist. Some so colorful I'd cut them into pieces and tie them around my ankles or wrists. I wore them in my hair, around my neck, like a "doo-rag," like a peasant, like a pioneer, like a bandit.

Tommy Christian, who wasn't, always asked if I'd won an Oscar yet—so I got grounded for telling him where he could put an Oscar and my mom seemed to think I shouldn't even know where adults tell other people to put things when they're mad—

But Johnny—just stared. I don't think he thought I looked, you know, funny or weird. He just stared. So I got bold. I tied scarves together. I sewed them. I made patches and I watched him stare. I know I was "showing" but I didn't care. Some people stare and you want to hit them. Johnny stared and I just wanted to make sure there was something for him to look at.

Then he asked me. And when he asked me, it seemed too simple—like maybe he wasn't who I thought he was: "Why do you wear those scarves like that all the time?"

Why did he have to ask? Didn't he know? I took two days to answer him. Then I walked up to him just after American History and smiled and said, "I'm a pirate." I don't know why I said it. I'd never played at being a pirate or anything. I saw the Johnny Depp movie and I'd been on that ride at Disneyland when I was five or something, but it wasn't like me to tell a story or say I was anything but me.

Then we were in Worlds of Food class and he was staring again. Just staring, like he didn't believe me, like he didn't care, and he looked me right in the eye.

"A pirate?"

I didn't know what he meant. But I had an apple in front of me. An apple and a knife. So I took a chance. I took the apple and looked him straight in the eye and then tossed the apple up in the air. In a swift motion I jabbed the knife straight up, and I guess some Greek goddess or something was helping me out because it went right into the heart of the apple. The apple just stuck there. I looked at Johnny, turned the apple over and jammed it down onto the cutting board where it split in half. And then I just smiled at him.

He doesn't talk to me much, but he still stares—only there's something different about it. I don't know if he's scared of me or if he likes me. Someday maybe I'll figure it out, but for now, I'll wear the scarves and I'll keep "showing."

ARE YOU WITH ME?
By Marcia Cebulska

(On April 23, 1951, at age 16, Barbara Rose Johns led a strike against her segregated and inadequately supported high school in Farmville, Virginia. The uprising led to one of the five cases that together went to the Supreme Court as **Brown v. Board of Education**, *resulting in the 1954 decision which overturned legalized segregation. This monologue is based on interviews with fellow strikers and Barbara Johns' own diary from the period.)*

Barbara

Every morning I get on a bus thrown away by the white high school on the hill. I sit on a torn seat and look out a broken window. And when my bus passes the shiny new bus that the white high-schoolers have, I hide my face because I'm embarrassed in my raggedy bus. And when we get to R.R. Moton High, the bus driver gets off with us, because he's also our history teacher. He comes in the classroom and fires up the stove and I sit in my winter coat waiting for the room to get warm. You know the rooms, the ones in the "addition" as they call it. We call them "the tar-paper shacks" because that's what they are, am I right?

I'm embarrassed that I go to school in tar-paper shacks and when it rains I have to open an umbrella so the leaks from the roof won't make the ink run on my paper. And

150

later in the day I have a hygiene class out in that bro-ken-down bus and a biology class in a corner of the audi-torium with one microscope for the whole school. I'm em-barrassed that our water fountains are broken and our wash basins are broken and it seems our whole school is broken and crowded and poor.

And I'm embarrassed.

But my embarrassment is nothing compared to my hunger. I'm not talking about my hunger for food. No, I'm hungry for those shiny books they have up at Farmville High. I want the page of the Constitution that is torn out of my social studies book. I want a chance at that *Romeo and Juliet* I've heard about but they tell me I'm not fit to read.

Our teachers say we can fly just as high as anyone else. That's what I want to do. Fly just as high. I said, fly.

You know, I've been sitting in my embarrassment and my hunger for so long that I forgot about standing up. So, to-day, I'm going to ask you to stand with me. Before we fly, before we fly just as high as anyone else, we gotta walk just as proud as anyone else. And that's what we're going to do! We're gonna walk out of this school and over to the courthouse. Do you hear me? We're gonna walk with our heads high and go talk to the school board.

Are you with me?

We're gonna walk out in a strike, yes, I said strike, and we won't come back until we get a real school with a gymna-sium and library and whole books. And we will get them.

And it'll be grand. Are you with me? Are we gonna walk? Are we gonna fly?

ARE YOU WITH ME? is excerpted from **Now Let Me Fly**, commissioned by the Brown Foundation for the 50th anniversary of the Supreme Court decision, **Brown v. Board of Education**. It was written while the author was playwright-in-residence at the William Inge Theatre Festival and was performed at 48 venues across the country in 2004, including the National Constitution Center and the National Center for the Study of Civil Rights.

CAMPAIGN RACE
By Joanna Leigh Congalton

(AVA is in high school and is running for student body president. She is relatively unpopular and is running against the quarterback of the football team. One day at lunch, she starts talking to a bunch of people about the upcoming elections.)

Ava

Hey guys, you know what would be really cool? A four-day school week. We go to school from ten a.m. to six p.m., Monday through Thursday. We'd be in school for something like eight hours a day, but we'd get a longer lunch and have Fridays off! Every weekend would be three days long. In order to get something like that done I'd have to win the school election. It would be nice to have someone as president who could make a difference. Do you guys know what's for lunch today? I heard it was fish sticks and cold gravy again. You know what would be nice?

Fresh, hot, pizza!

I'm sure that if the president of the school suggested that we order pizza once a week, the school board would listen. But you'd need a president who knew how to work the school board. Did I mention that my uncle is on the school board? Anyway, I just had a great idea. We should get the new school president to bring back recess. Remember back in elementary school when we'd get a half-hour break between classes to go outside? It would fit perfectly into that four-day school-week schedule I was telling you guys about. It would be great to have some time off during the day aside from lunch. You could study for a test or catch up on homework or just chill out with your friends.

Why stop there?

I think that every student with a license should get his or her own spot in the faculty parking lot. Our parents are the ones paying taxes for us to be here, how come we have to park a block or more away? Then who's to stop us from getting school uniforms? We could all look alike. You won't have to worry about picking out clothes in the morning or...wait, where are you guys going?

Don't walk away!

I haven't even told you about carnival day yet and I thought you wanted to get uniforms; they would make your hair stand out more. Come back, guys! OK, forget about the uniforms. We could still get four days of school a week if you...guys? Wait up, did I tell you what's for lunch today?

WAR

By Mike Thomas

(PETE, an intelligent, sensitive young teenager, is questioning the politics of war and the media and growing up in a world that fights all the time.)

Pete

It was a pretty crappy day at school. Randy Wyman called me a "mama's boy" at P.E. in front of everybody and I didn't do anything about it. He's a jerk. Then walking home from school, I saw these kids fighting in the alley. All big kids, older high school maybe. I hid behind this old fence at the corner of the alley and watched 'cause I heard the yelling. It looked like this one dark-haired kid had beat up this other kid and he was standing over him yelling and spitting on him.

Then suddenly two other guys came up and started beating up on him, the guy standing, you know. I guess they were friends of the guy on the ground. All I really know is it was a fight. They hit and kicked him for a long time it seemed. He tried to fight back, but there were two of them. I heard weird sounds I had never heard before; cracking and popping sounds...bones, I think. I saw the guy spit out blood and I felt kinda numb and sick. Part of me was like, "go break that up, why are you hiding?" And another part was kinda scared. I couldn't watch. I turned and ran. I didn't do anything. Why didn't I yell or something? I've never been in a fight. I can usually talk my way out of 'em.

Why didn't I try to stop the fight?

When I got home I turned on the television. The news. Nothing but war and violence. This country and that country. Our country. In history class every section of American History ends with a war. This country was built on war. But I am constantly told how bad fighting is. "Solve your problems by talking it out. Don't resort to your fists." Even my karate teacher says, "the best thing about learning karate is never having to use it."

Why didn't I stop that fight?

At school when a fight breaks out, everyone yells, "C'mon, get him. Hit him." I walk away and try to find a teacher. Sometimes I'm the only one. Am I some kind of wuss for not wanting to fight? It feels right but I feel like a freak. I've been watching the news since I was five and I worry…a lot when I watch the news. I can't take my eyes off of it, but I can't turn off the channel. I feel like it just goes on and on and there is nothing I can do.

I couldn't shut Randy Wyman up, I couldn't stop that fight in the alley, and I can't help all the starving children, and I can't stop a war, so get over it. It just kills me. We gotta say something. Somebody's got to stop this somehow, sometime.

I can't do it all.

RIDING ON THE HEAD OF A DRAGON
By Elizabeth Wong

(KUAN YIN is a teenage girl who lives at the intersection of reality and mythology. She has long flowing white hair and is dressed in white Chinese robes with floor-length sleeves. She stands at the top of a magnificent sweeping red staircase.)

Kuan Yin

I am standing on the head of a dragon, riding the waves toward my destination, the threshold of heaven. In my right hand, a sacred willow branch, I use it to sprinkle nectar upon the heads of the wounded and heartsick. In my left hand, The Sutra, the Dharma—words of truth—as spoken by the lips of the great teacher Buddha. But the book is lost; I cannot find it. But, well, truth is always hard to find, isn't it?

It's not easy to balance on the head of a dragon.

Have you ever wondered why some dreams come to you again and again? They are urgent messages from your true self, beacons of remembrance, gentle elbows to nudge nudge wink wink you awake from your amnesia. It always starts this way. I find a key inside a red envelope inside a drawer of my desk. I am riding on the head of a dragon. I try to give the key to you, but you won't take it. When I was a little girl, and not a goddess, my daddy asked me to go to the store with him, to buy some ice cream, but I was so busy playing with my friends. Sleepover! I love sleepovers! He asked me what kind of ice cream? Get vanilla, Daddy. We want vanilla! Daddy wanted me to go with him, but I didn't go, because I was building a fort out of pillows and blankets with my friends.

We were building a fort with pillows and blankets. Making tunnels and secret hiding places with pillows and blankets, old cardboard boxes. We ate vanilla ice cream cones and went to bed inside our fort of pillows and blankets. When we were all asleep. Daddy fell off the bed. I heard the *thud* like it was thunder. Mommy is screaming, James James James wake up James. Next thing I know, I see Daddy in a box and Mommy is crying. I hate vanilla ice cream, vanilla ice cream makes me so sad. My father wanted me to go to the store with him. No, no thanks, Pop, I want to build a fort with my friends.

I ate his ice cream while he was dying inside. That's all I remember.

But that was another life. I tell you this because I want you to know I understand your loss, your pain. The truth of our father, forever lost. But now I am a goddess. Riding on the waves, on the head of a dragon, coming to rescue you.

Take my hand.

Take it.

JENNY'S WISH
By Mike Thomas

(JENNY is appealing to her father to let her follow her passion.)

Jenny

Can you please just listen a minute? It's something I really want to do. Why can't you just accept that? It's not like someone is going to get hurt if this is not the right choice for me. Let me make my own mistakes. That's how I learn, right? But you think *I*—that I'm such a "perfect" little girl that I will do whatever you say in the end, even if I truly believe you're wrong. Here's how I played it in my mind. I was going to say,

(Playing the dutiful daughter.)

"Dad you are so smart and you have lived so long…"

(Editing herself.)

No…strike that…"lived so long" part. "Dad you are so smart that I will respect whatever you say." And then you're supposed to say,

(Imitating her dad.)

"Well, Jenny, that is such a sign of respect and maturity, that I now say that you can make your own choices in life from this point on." But you're not saying that! I've done the cheerleader thing, Dad, and it's not me. I just want to join a dance class. I've always loved dancing and watching dancers. They are strong and graceful and elegant and beautiful. It's like poetry.

Do you remember when Mom dragged us to this play, and you said you didn't want to go to the "theatre." There was some big game on, but you went with us anyway. It was this old Russian play. I was about twelve and there was this beautiful dance number, this scene between these people in a ballroom. I know you remember...and there were three men and three women and they flew through the air and landed with a softness you couldn't hear, like angel's feet. They leapt high and twisted and turned and carried each other and looked at each other and...they spoke to me, Dad, without saying a word. I can't tell you the name of the play but I have never forgotten that dance. It was the most beautiful thing I have ever seen. That's when I knew...I was born to dance.

And don't be mad at me but...every Tuesday after school...I've been watching Ms. Rosemary's dance class. She lets me sit in the back. There are eleven girls and they are just learning, but by watching them I'm learning, too. I watch the girls for an hour and then practice in our garage before you get home.

I want to dance for you, Dad. Tomorrow when you come home, I want you to sit in a lawn chair in the driveway. I'll hit the CD player and the garage door will open and I'll show you how much I've learned and what dancing means to me. Then you'll have to say yes. It takes discipline and strength and art and you can tell a story with it. You'll see. You'll be so overcome with emotion at how beautiful... and graceful...and elegant your daughter can be. You'll see me and I'll be just like the people in that ballroom.

Will you watch?

DESERT DREAMS
By Ellen Fairey

(EDIE, 13, climbs onto an overturned washing machine in her backyard in El Paso, Texas. It is dusk.)

Edie

My mom needs quiet when she meditates…so I come sit out here. We moved to El Paso last summer, right before I started eighth grade. Mom says the heat's good for you, "the sun heals," so we bought this used convertible Beetle Bug and drove almost the whole way here with the top down. It was like a hundred degrees and totally noisy but it didn't matter because all that wind made her look like she was smiling.

I guess she's right about the sun and the heat thing, because before, in Michigan, she used to stay in bed all day reading catalogs and staring into space. Now she does stuff that's for her "Self," like transcendental meditation and burning incense.

Dad's still in Michigan. Mom says he has a problem discussing his feelings, among other things, and that she was sick of trying to guess what was going on in his mind. She says basically he's a good person, it's just that he would be perfectly happy doing nothing but going to work, coming home and watching "M*A*S*H" for the rest of his life and she wanted more. I told her that I liked "M*A*S*H" and that I had even written a fan letter to

161

Hawkeye once and gotten a postcard back that said: "Be Cool, Stay in School." She just rolled her eyes and said, "I'm glad Hawkeye is so pro-education, that's very reassuring." I'm pretty sure she wasn't really glad, and that somehow the fact that I watched "M*A*S*H" made her even angrier at Dad.

It's not like she's an expert at discussing her feelings. Half the time you don't know if she's happy or sad or what, and then all of a sudden she's throwing a jade plant on the floor saying "I can't take this anymore!" and you have no idea what happened. Or why.

This morning I saw her looking at the photo album of when we lived in Michigan. She was turning the pages like if she wasn't careful they might break. When she saw me she told me it was supposed to rain. She said "just in time, thank God, before we all dry up and turn into tumbleweeds." I'm thinking: I know, let's get out of here, let's go back to Michigan where there's trees and lakes and water and no desert. *(Pause.)* ...let's go back to Dad.

But I didn't say anything.

I just rubbed her shoulders the way she likes and gave her some space.

THE NEATNESS FACTOR
By Nancy Gall-Clayton

(LEE desperately seeks the order and calm of the library over the troubling chaos of life.)

Lee

That's why I want a job at the library—because of the neatness factor. My dad's a packrat, and my mom hates housework, so where I live is like a dusty, messy warehouse. Here everything is so uncluttered, so tidy, so *in place*. Even the newspapers are lined up on special metal shelves, from the *Atlanta Constitution* to the *Washington Post*. And, oh! I love the fold-back part of the shelf where you keep last week's papers.

At home we have lots of papers, too—*Indianapolis Stars*—but they're definitely not organized. They're in stacks higher than my waist—in the living room, the kitchen, the back porch, even the bathtub! Dad is convinced he'll be able to sell them if he has a whole ton. He says they'll take his old *Motor Trend*s and Mom's *Redbook*s, too, but I'm not so sure. I'm not sure they'll take any of it, but just in case, I have my subscription to *National Wildlife* sent to my cousin's address, and that's the only place I read anything important.

That's what makes me right for this library job. I'm a planner, and I care about order. My bedroom is so clean you wouldn't believe a fifteen-year-old lives there. I moved all my clothes into the bureau, so my share of Dad's newspapers is stuffed in the closet and under my bed. Also, I know my alphabet extremely well because I had an alphabet video when I was little. I had other videos, too, but one by one, they got lost in newspapers, and I wound up listening to the alphabet one about five hundred times before I turned six. I will never get Judy Blume and Lillian Jackson Braun in the wrong order or T.H. White and E.B. White. I know that mostly helps with fiction, but isn't that one of your specialties?

Anyway, I'm just perfect for the job, and the job's perfect for me. How about it?

Can I work here?

THE GOOD FIGHT
By Claudia Haas

(RANDY [or RANDI], 15, is furious with his mother.)

Randy

I'm so mad at you, Mom! Do you realize what you're doing to your own kid? Why are you clipping news reports about people who don't wear helmets on motorcycles and shoving them in my face every morning? What's with this collecting statistical information on auto accidents? I wake up to a bowl of cereal on my right and a story of "Death on Our Roadways Today" on my left. What kind of a wake-up call do you think that is? Do you really want me start each day in "The Land of Negativity"?

(As the mother.)

"I won't let you go behind the wheel, Randy, unless I know you can control your temper." Temper, what temper? You do know, of course, that *all* my friends are driving. *All* my friends will have their license by the summer.

(As the mother.)

"I don't care about all of your friends. I only care about you!" Don't care so much, Mom! Pick on someone your own age! Pick on Dad! You're choking me with your worries, Mom. Take me off the leash! I'm not your pet. You look at me and say, "I don't know who you are anymore."

You know, I can say the same thing. We don't yell at each other anymore. We don't even talk. There's barely a whisper between us. To tell you the truth, I miss the yelling. I mean, you could be pretty scary sometimes. We'd both just get so fierce when we defended our own point of view. You're always trying to keep me so safe and I'm always trying to take a chance.

But now you do more than protect—you're like the "Voice of Doom." Everything is bad for me. Mouthwash is a carcinogenic. Rock music makes me deaf. Video games bring on epilepsy. You serve me a daily dose of ways the modern world is killing me. And the worst thing is—I can't fight back. I can't get mad at you. I want to. You know I want to. And that's what really scares me. Your long list of ways the world can hurt me doesn't frighten me a bit, Mom. It's you. You've given up the fight. You're tired, I know. You're sick.

But you have to know I'm wondering—where is my mother?

I want to go back—just a couple of weeks before the treatments...before the surgery...before the "routine" checkup. Put yourself at the kitchen table reading a newspaper. Now turn to the Letters to the Editor and start reading. There's always one that makes your blood boil. Remember getting all riled up and angry? Do you remember how that felt? I want to see that fiery person I've been locked in battle with all my life. I need you to fight for yourself. I've brought you pills; I've brought you dinner, and now, Mom, I'm bringing the newspaper. And I'm going to read some of those Letters to the Editor to you.

I'm going to read the most closed-minded, ignorant ones I can find. I'm going to find ways to irritate you and annoy you until you are furious. And you're going to use that anger and fight for yourself, Mom. I need you to take up the struggle. This time for yourself. Will you at least put up a fight? 'Cause when you have this thing licked and you're back in full force, we can go back to our sparring ways.

I need that. It's the only way I can figure things out for myself.

BACK OF THE BUS
By Joanna Leigh Congalton

(TED [or TEDDIE] takes the bus to school daily, is always the first one on and the last one off. And sits alone.)

Ted

Look at them, I bet they're all thinking "there's Ted, he's so weird. He has no friends. All he ever does is read. Why does he always sit in the back? He's a loser!" Well, what do they know? They never invite me to sit with them, so why should they care where I sit? It's not like they ever talk to me. But that doesn't matter. If it did then it would get to me, the way that they all look at the empty seat next to me, every time they get on the bus. The way nobody ever sits there. They never look at me, just the seat, like it's contaminated. Like they'll catch whatever I have, whatever makes me so different.

Maybe there's something wrong with me, and I just don't know about it. Like the story in that book, the one where the boy's invisible but he doesn't know it. He thinks everybody is just ignoring him. He doesn't know it's because they can't see him. That's got to be it…

No, it can't be.

If I was invisible then the bus wouldn't pull up to my stop every day. Maybe I smell and nobody ever told me be-

168

cause the stench is so horrible that they can't bear to get close to me... No, that can't be it either. My parents would have said something to me about it years ago. What if my parents smell just like I do? Maybe I live on top of a landfill? No, that's not something you can ignore. Maybe I should just ask them why nobody sits next to me.

Who am I kidding?

I'd rather just sit here and keep wondering. I'll read my books and watch them stare. I'll just sit here because I don't care what they think. Just look at them all sitting in their seats, talking to their friends. Maybe I'm the normal one. Did they ever think of that? No, probably not... I just wish I knew what made me so different. Why do I have to sit alone? Why can't anyone ever come and sit next to me? I'll tell you why. It's because I like reading my books and I like being alone. But sometimes I wouldn't mind having someone sit next to me. Someone to talk to about books maybe or about sports, the weather, anything.

What am I saying? I don't need them. I don't need anyone.

I have time to read and I like the quiet back here, but maybe, someday...

I'll sit next to one of them.

BRAIN FREEZE
By Kerri Kochanski

(TERRY, an eager but highly nervous teenager, is getting up the courage to ask for a date.)

Terry

Brain freeze... Sometimes my head gets all mushy and I have a brain freeze... Like I can't think of things... Like I am sitting here trying to think of things...but I *can't* think of things... You *know...?* You know how that *feels...?* Like you are trying to think of something— *Any*thing *interest*ing... But you can't think at all... It's like your brain got locked... Like you were listening to a tape recorder and you *pressed pause*—you pressed the pause button... *You* are the pause button... Am I making any sense...?

Because sometimes I think I don't make sense and it makes me feel like other people don't want to listen to me but I *know* what I have to say is important and I *know* other humans must feel this because *I* am human and human beings experience the *same things*— I mean it's not like I'm an alien and *no human being* could ever experience what I've experienced before—we have a *connec-*tion. A *common ground.*

I mean, you do under*stand*, don't you...? Because if you didn't under*stand*...

Well, then I would have to think I was *crazy*. *I'm* crazy.
This—
(Indicates their interaction.)
is crazy. Because you don't just go up to people and *start
talk*ing... *Start talking*... When you have absolutely *noth-
ing*... Nothing of value to *say*...
(Wonders, probes.)
Do you...? I mean I know *I* do... But do *you*... Do you...
ever do this...? Sit here and talk...? About nothing...?
(Pretends to enjoy self.)
It's nice, isn't it...
(Indicating nothing.)
This, is nice...

Okay it's really not that nice. I *still* don't know what to
tell you...! My brain...! It's frozen...! And I don't know
what to say. Really, I don't know what to say.

You want an icepop?

RIPPER GIRL
By Elizabeth Wong

(CASSIE, late teens, has a well-used banged-up skate-board with lots of stickers affixed.)

Cassie

We don't date. Kids my age, we hang out. We just kick it. So basically, if you want a boyfriend, it's not like he asks you out. Guys just corner you at some party, and if you suck face, that's it. No one gets all that formal. I tried having a boyfriend once, but I got sick of waitin' by the phone for him to call, so I just grabbed my board, and headed out to a place I heard about, down by the culvert. It's a dried-out drainage pipe, a really cool find.

I heard some of the biggest rip dogs come down here, but no one was around. Had the pipe all to myself. Which was fine with me. I'm alone a lot. Which is fine. I'm not what you call popular, and like, well, I'm pretty dumb. Stupid actually, that's what my father says when he sees my report cards.
(Deftly, she flips up her board with her foot, and catches it.)
I was gettin' into my style. I was in a groove, and feelin' no pain. This pipe was so sweet. So I got kinda bold. I tried for a goofy foot tailgrab and totally missed big time. Heard this sick pop. Like the bone here is sticking out, and I'm freakin'.

172

Then this guy, like from nowhere, like out of thin air, like some crazy-ass angel, comes running up to me. I'm holding my leg like this. Dude goes, "You were rad. For a girl, you have this awesome rubber-band style." I go, "Shut up." He goes, "You're gonna be okay, don't talk, okay?" I go, "Just shut up." He goes, "I was up there watchin', you were awesome." I go, "You thought so?" He goes, "Absolutely. And oh, by the way, I called 911." I go, "I'm gonna pass out." He goes, "You should tighten your nuts. Your trucks are loose."

On the way to the hospital, he tightens my bushings. Which was prime; coolest thing anyone has ever done for me. I woke up in the ambulance, dude was sitting next to me. He goes, "What's your name, girl?" I go, "Cassie, I think." "Well Cassie, I'm Curtis. And you are gonna be okay to rip another day, so lay back and let these good folks do their thing, okay?" So I lay back.

Every time our eyes met, he just really looked at me. Like no one ever looked before. I didn't just disappear into nothing. I could even see my reflection. In the hospital, I told Curtis stuff I normally just keep to myself. Like how I'm not very good at baking cookies, or doing geometry, or makin' friends. Like how my mom died, and I miss her so much. And like how my father married this person who looks like my mom but who isn't. How like the only time I feel things go right for me, is when I'm riding my skateboard. When I'm rippin', I feel like I'm a genius.

And you know what? Curtis? He was a good listener too. And after I was done with my litany of self-loathing, dude said, "Cassie, I'm gonna come back tomorrow, and tomorrow, and when you get out of here, I'm gonna visit you at your house. If that's all right with you. And, oh, here's some flowers. I got 'em from the gift store downstairs in between times when you were passed out cold."

(She flips up board, hugs it.)

Flowers. I didn't know what to say. Which was typical. But Curtis didn't seem to care. This totally cool cute guy, a complete stranger, gave me flowers.

(Smiles shyly.)

Daisies.

SAMANTHA'S PLIGHT
By Mike Thomas

(SAMANTHA is sitting outside the principal's office. She is seated next to a kid much younger than she is and decides to tell her side to explain her version of the story.)

Samantha

I have to see the principal because everybody in this school thinks I'm a jinx. You know what a jinx is? It's a witch's voodoo curse. Every time we all play kickball or football or baseball, the team I'm on loses. So they switch me and then that team loses. Last Friday I was in right-field...the ball is coming right at me and I pass out, it was a hundred degrees. Has anyone heard of sunstroke?

I'm standing in line last Saturday afternoon getting ready to get a ticket to one of those *Lord of the Rings* sequels. And suddenly the guy in front of me is searching all of his pockets like this.
(She demonstrates patting her pockets.)
Then I hear him say he lost ten dollars. "I've lost my money, I've lost my money!" He says it must have fallen out of his pocket and he turns around and looks right at me. I just smiled and went—
(She shrugs her shoulders.)
—with my hands open, you know? He just shook his head like he knew I took it. What's that about? I am not bad

luck, and I didn't take his ten dollars. I really didn't. And I didn't cause him to lose it either. But I felt like I did.

Sometimes I jinx myself. I always say the wrong thing. That's the worst. This one boy, let's call him John to protect the innocent. Well, John asks me to go to this dance thing at school. No big deal but he is kinda cute and he's in real good with Mr. Baldwin, the math teacher, and he's in the "100 percent club." Anyway, we're in the hallway by the lockers and he comes up and asks me to this dance in the gym, and I'm not positive but I think I said: "Ummm Who...go with...what you?...dance'em"... I mean I couldn't speak! He just looks at me and he knows I'm a long way from Gifted and Talented. I never got to the dance.

And now, in last period, Ricky Jenkins passes the "I've Got Diarrhea May I Please Leave?" sign up to the teacher. He's just messin' with the sub and everyone's laughing but of course the sign ends up on my desk! How did that happen? And when the substitute comes by and sees the sign and then looks at me, I mean the joke's over.
(Getting angry.)
I start yelling "I don't have diarrhea." *(Poking herself in the stomach.)* "Do I look like I have diarrhea? Ricky Jenkins has diarrhea, not me!"

So, here I am again, waiting for my punishment. I want to just get it over with so I can "move on," you know? Man, I hope this jinx thing doesn't follow me my whole life. One of these days when this all balances out, I'm going to be the luckiest person in the world. Like this morning on the way to school a squirrel ran across the street right in front of us and made it!

We didn't kill it!

Now that's pretty lucky, don't you think? But until then, you might not want to sit too close to me.

LIKE LIGHTING A CANDLE
By Christa Kreimendahl

(ANGIE, a pregnant woman under the age of 19, enters the living room of her mobile home. She struggles to set up a tripod and video camera which she places down front. She then plops herself into a rocking chair facing the camera. She's nervous but manages a smile and a wave.)

Angie

Hi, Baby Sara.
(She rubs her stomach.)
I'm Angie...your mommy, and I love you very much. *(Silence.)* I've been waitin' 'til you was far enough along that you'd make it, because they have this procedure that they can do, I seen it on TV. If somethin' happens t' the momma then they can just take you right out, right outta me.

I gotta make this video for ya 'cause there's not a lot of time and I might not be here t' tell you all a' the things you're gonna need t' know. Like...well, first off, don't you take any crap from no one. It ain't gonna be easy growin' up here in this trailer park. People are gonna try an' hurt you. You gotta growl a lot and be loud. And make sure you know someone real good before you let them get too close. And, baby girl—the boys in this trailer park ain't no good for you. No matter what lies they talk. That's exactly what they are...lies.

178

You stay away from the drugs and the drinkin', especially that crack-cocaine. Those two trailers at the end of the road up here... *(Pointing.)* Don't you go up there, and don't be socializin' with any a' them folks. It'll take you and everything you love away from you. Before you know it, you'll be gettin' near t' thirty, skinnier than Mrs. Jewels in trailer C, and you'll be doin' all the things that women do when they need t' get what they need t' get. I seen it out there. Some things are real ugly.

Even people you love can turn ugly. I don't want you t' see your momma turn. I had hopes. I did. I used to feel like I had somethin' t' offer. Now, it seems like the more I struggle to get back t' that girl I was—the further I get away from it. I get scared when I think about you bein' in my arms. *(Beat.)* You can't trust me... I don't want nothin' t' ever happen to my baby girl. And I sure don't wanna be the one t' hurt you. Babies shouldn't be hurt by their own mommas.
(With enthusiasm and energy.)
Next, you gotta make sure you stay in school, Sara. My daughter is gonna graduate from high school, you hear me? Don't you let no one hold you back because a' where you come from. Don't you let no one, no one make you feel stupid. A lot a' people done come up from a gutter that's dirtier than yours. You can be a great person! Don't you let them tell you you can't, because as soon as you do...that's it. It's all over. That's what happened t' these people 'round here. They believed the lie, Sara. They believed that this—that this is it. Yes, that's why this place is what it is.

But there's some good stuff here, too. You always gotta find somethin' good. Like a ladybug in your hair—just a little button from heaven. Or Mr. Jim's got the barbeque goin' and a few a' the teenagers waitin' for a chance t' sample the goods. Or Tony, white-haired and just a rockin' away in his chair, wavin' at every single person that goes by 'cause it makes him feel good.

(Beat. She's exhausted and frightened.)

God—there's jus' so much t' tell you. So much. A whole lifetime a' stuff! Your father, sometimes he gets his feathers ruffled. He's got him a hot temper, but you just wait it out. A few moments time he's as sweet as mango nectar. He tells me that I shouldn't worry about me hurtin' you. He said that God don't make no mistakes. He tells me that I got this life growin' inside a' me 'cause things are gonna turn around. He tells me I ain't gotta worry no more, that mommas don't hurt their babies. He don't understand that even people you love turn ugly. When he says these things t' me sometimes I feel like, yeah, yeah maybe he's right. Maybe somethin' happens when you give life to a baby.

Like lightin' a candle in a church.

A prayer.

Maybe things change for the good. I wanna believe that. I do. It's gotta be true. But I…I gotta get this camera back or they'll charge me extra for— I love you, Sara. I can almost see you smilin'. I can. I really can.

(ANGIE turns off the tape.)

NOT ON THIS EARTH
By Kevin M. Lottes

(CHRIS, late teens, is seated in the front seat of his car. A packed suitcase is on the passenger seat. He is confused and angered by his indecision.)

Chris

What on earth is stopping me from jumping into my car and driving clear on up, all the way to Indy, to pull you out of that city mess and drag you, by the hair if I have to, back home with me where you belong? What could possibly be holding me back? I think about it all the time.

I exercise the thought as if it was the only thought I possessed. And man, what a possession this sort of imagination presents to itself: this image of rescuing someone you love from something you think is the wrong way to go. I guess I have a fear of finding out exactly how you might react to something so hopelessly romantic. Or maybe I know deep down, all the way through the heart of the matter, if I did say something silly like, "Hey, I love you! Now you're coming with me!" that you wouldn't accept it. You would crawl into a little ball in the corner, leaving nothing for me to latch onto, and you would squeeze the life out of my testimony to you, and how I really feel about you right now.

I think about you as if you were dead and I loved only the memory of you, but you're alive! You're alive! And so am

I! And I wonder why the hell you wouldn't want to wave a white flag and surrender to me—just give it up! I'm begging you! I would come to you before your next heartbeat and you know it. A picture of you is in motion and my mind has no time for anything else right now. Oh hell—what do I have to lose: Hey, I love you! Now pack your bags, flush that trash down the toilet, and get your shoes on. You're coming home with me!

I CHANGED MY MIND
By Nancy Gall-Clayton

(RUTHIE explains to her mother why she has decided not to have her birthmark removed.)

Ruthie

I changed my mind, Mama. I don't want the operation after all. It's not because of the doctor. I like her a lot, and I trust her. It's not because I'm scared of being operated on. I am a little scared, but that's logical and normal, don't you think, it's an *operation*. It's not because of the insurance either. Uncle Joe can afford to pay the difference, and he promised to long ago. He doesn't have kids, and he always likes doing special things for me that are hard for us to afford.

Honest, it's not because of anything except me.

From the time I understood what mirrors were and started looking into them, I've always seen a blonde-haired girl with a smile and an upturned nose and then, on the left cheek, a birthmark that looks like a flash of purple lightning. I know this girl. She has a big aquarium full of goldfish, and she takes tumbling lessons. She wins spelling bees, and she's good at math. Her best friend is named Janie, and she and Janie ride their bikes on the trail down by the river every Saturday. You'll probably say the operation will only change one thing, but I think you're wrong.

If my face looks different, won't I be different?

And here's what does scare me. Other people will be different. I won't be able to figure out who likes me for real. Even now, kids whisper about me. Some kids look at me funny and even point, but you know what? My birthmark saves me the trouble of figuring out who's nice and who isn't. I know you think I'm too young to be sure about a big decision like not having the operation. I know the doctor said now was a good time, but Mama, what if I accidentally married a man who didn't love the real me? Wouldn't that be way, way worse than a purple birthmark?

Don't you think it's better for me to just be me?

ONE MORE CHANCE
By Mike Thomas

(JAKE, 15, broke up with his girlfriend six months ago. But he can't get her out of his mind. And he's not doing particularly well in his English class either.)

Jake

I really can't believe her. You try to please somebody... bring 'em flowers, buy 'em CD's and crap, tell 'em you love 'em and it's still not enough. You think you know someone after six months and then they pull the plug. We were joined at the hip. But I guess that's over. She made the bed now she can live in it or lay in it...or is it lie? And she lied to me, too. I caught her in more than one lie. She's a liar but I still stayed with her.

That was not her cousin!

We grew up together, had some good times. I took her to the county fair. One of those early, cool September nights and the Ferris wheel stopped us at the top and, man, she could kiss. She nearly ripped that little thing that hangs in the back of your throat outta me. Boy, she loved to kiss. I loved that about her. But she loved to fight, too, and I have had enough of that, so it is over. *(Sigh.)* Boy, she smelled good. One of my jackets still smells like her. I guess I'll have to burn it. A person can only take so much, you know?

So I said goodbye to her and her smell.

We met on a church camping trip, but she didn't act like no Christian I ever knew. We took a long walk in the woods that night, we sat by a little pond and talked all night. Just held each other, kissed a little and it was just great. I need that. But she has broken all my straws...or her straws...or the camel's back...or...whatever.

Whatever we had, it's gone!

I'm not one to blame somebody else but it really is all her fault. It's too late for any making up now. When someone's had enough...it's enough. I mean we had fun, but fun spelled backwards is "nuf." So I pretty much wipe my hands on her...uh. Wash 'em...of her. If she's gonna treat me like this then I will just return the favor and she can put that in her hat and smoke it.

(He pathetically needs her back in his life.)
If she can just say the word I'd give her one more chance, isn't that sick? I'd give her one more chance. Well, maybe.

THE INFORMATION BOOTH
by Lucinda McDermott

(BOBBY [or BOBBIE] approaches an information booth at an amusement park.)

Bobby

Excuse me, sir. Sir!…yes! *No!* Over here! *Down* here… yes! Thank you. I would like some information if you please. I mean the sign says "Information," right? Okay then! Uh…well, I was just wondering: is car sickness contagious? See, we just got here and the whole way up my cousin Katherine threw up all over the place. Yeah, gross-a-licious. She's thirteen and should be over that by now, don't you think?… Yeah, me too.

What? Oh yeah, I'm getting to that.

See, after my dad paid for us to get into the park I started running toward the Thunder Bolt of Terror. Whoa. Way cool ride. Have you ridden it? So you know what I'm talking about. Sweet, huh? Well anyways, I get off, and like my parents are M.I.A…Missing In Action…come on, keep up, and…*What?!* Of course I'm not lost. It's my parents that are lost. I'm right here, at the Information Booth. Get your lenses checked, four eyes!

Sorry. Sorry about that. No need to be rude.

It's just that...I'm worried about my parents. Yeah. They uh, they're not good in crowds, you know? Hey, maybe they're in trouble. Maybe they got stuck on a ride—or maybe they fell off the log flume and no one can save them...what? How dare you suggest that I'm scared. What nerve. What audacity. Look, guacamole brain; I make straight A's. I'm a model child and my teachers love me. I acolyte twice a month at All Angels Episcopal Church. Scared? Lost? Me? The idea. The very idea. You make me laugh.

Ha ha. Me lost. How very funny.

Don't you see, I'm merely concerned for my parents. So, please—please get on your loudspeaker and page them? Okay. "Mom and Daaaaaa..." I mean, "Mr. and Mrs. Jeffries." Tell them I'm concerned about their where-abouts, and...and...I will be waiting for them at the Information Booth.

Oh. Thanks. Thanks a lot.

COMING TO

By Rosemary McLaughlin

(REBECCA has just survived an automobile accident. She examines her surroundings, her hands, how she is standing. She is bright, curious and trying to get her bearings.)

Rebecca

There's this picture I can't get out of my head: spider web. Windshield. There's a spider web in the wind... No. That's not it.

(Pause.)

Wind-through-the-shield. Spider veins! Fanning out like a pinwheel, my hair. Fanning out on the glass, fanning me, with the glass. Toward the glass? The glass-towards-me?

(Breathlessly.)

The glass towards me—not me don't do that! The glass towards me and the spiders they're coming on glass legs they're creaking spies.

(Catching her breath.)

It's just a picture. It's just a picture.

(Steadying herself.)

But I can't get it out. I can't. Do-this. I can't do this this ticks me off I can't do this-this-this-stop!

(Breathes deliberately.)

Start over.

(She sighs.)

I was just looking out the window. I was drowsy. I saw the oil tanks, the oil rigs. At night they look like—they look like Trojans. No!

(Laughs.)

That's not it!

(Pause.)

A horse. At night. Two of them, flank to flank in the night waiting by the wall. Flames in their eyes. They do something with Arabian oil. Forty Thieves? In a Trojan horse?

(Rubs her head as if to clear it.)

It's not Troy. There's no dead Greeks. There's no wall there. There's a road.

(She sees it more clearly now.)

Three lanes—six lanes. They go this way and that. The lines in the web over my face.

(She sinks, knowing she's lost the sense of the picture.)

I can't take off this face my fingers have spiders in them red with strands tying me to my legs the seat the floor of the car the door the radio the glove compartment the flashlight falling out my gum the glass towards me the glass towards me I don't want it nooooo!

(Pause.)

Spiders make spider veins.

(Whispers.)

They make pictures.

(Pause.)

I don't want it.

(Sighs.)

Touching…what I miss.

GOTTA GET IT
By Cynthia Mercati

(CHRISTY is giving herself a pep talk as she approaches her locker. She wears a backpack.)

Christy

Get a plan. Get a start. Get a new start!
(She pulls out a mirror from her backpack, studying herself.)
Get a look. Get a new look.
(Feeling her face, worried.)
Get a zit? Get some cream.
(Planning.)
Get some lip gloss, get some blush, get some eyeliner. Get some mascara. Get that triple-enhancing, lash-extending, twenty-four-hour mascara!
(She fluffs her hair, debating.)
Get some mousse? Get some gel? Get some wax? Get some spray? Get some highlights!
(Giving herself another pep talk.)
Get organized. Get your homework done. Get it all done. Get it all done tonight. Get it all done right!
(She sits, deflated.)
Get smarter.
(A hopeful thought.)
Get smarter friends!
(She stands, planning again.)
Get some new friends. Get some cool friends.
(Suddenly aware of what she's wearing.)

191

Get some cool clothes.
  (Realizing the problem.)
Get some money.
  (Planning again.)
Get a job, get some money—get some clothes. Get some style. Get stylin'. Get a tattoo?
  (Shakes her head no. She sinks down on the bench again. Hopefully, she checks her phone.)
Get a call?
  (No call. She wishes.)
Get a call, get a call, get a call. Please, please, please, get a call.
  (Sternly.)
Get something better to say when you get a call.
  (She stands, trying out various ways to answer the phone.)
Hi!

Hi, there.

Hello, there.

Oh, hi.

Oh, like hi.
  (She's disgusted with every approach. Totally embarrassed, she sinks down on the bench.)
Get a clue.
  (Depressed.)
Get some Cheetos—get some Peanut Butter Cups. Get some Ho-Ho's.
  (She stands, going on with purpose—another plan.)

Get a better body. Get a firmer body. Get some abs. Get some boobs!

(She jogs in place.)

Get some weights. Get a workout! Get some workout clothes.

(The pace of her jogging increases, matching the tempo of her words.)

Get a grip, get a clue, get a look, get a life, get grades, get a guy, get a job, get a car, get cool—

(A sudden thought.)

Get your books.

(She jogs to her locker, tries to open it—it sticks. She pulls, she pounds—it sticks. She kicks it. It sticks.)

Get your locker open!!

PURITY
By Jett Parsley

(MARCUS is considering joining the Marines. He has recently returned from a social affair that has raised important questions concerning the nature of loyalty and manhood.)

Marcus

I thought twice about it, sure. When he first said where we were going. When the other guys started hooting. As we got out of the Jeep. As we walked toward the door. I thought about my options. I could suggest a different place. I could get sick. I could remember there was something I had to do. But really. What am I going to say? "Dude, I can't go in there, my mom would have a fit. You guys go in without me, I'm going to stay out here and read my Bible."

Right.

This is my *Marines* recruiter. These are guys I'm going to shoot guns with. They want to go in to some restaurant where the waitresses wear next to nothing and sit on your lap and—well, am *I* going to be the one to stop them?

Debbie said, "So you'll be all right then if *I* get a job down there?" I nearly exploded when she said that—not *my* girlfriend! Which was exactly the point she wanted to make. Man, I only told her because I thought she'd be the one to understand. I mean, *she* struggles with it—her girl-friends go out to the mall and buy those little tiny spa-ghetti-strap things that show the bra straps and Debbie wants one—shoot, Debbie *owns* one, but she knows her dad would have a fit, and she knows what God says, so she doesn't wear it. She says she's going to wear it just for me someday when we're married.

Which is what I was thinking when that lady was sitting on my lap. I was thinking about Debbie and her little spa-ghetti-strap thing that waits for me and the pledges we signed that night in church and how sick she'd be that I was looking at any other girl and how hard it is to wait when there's women like this who'll wear the spaghetti strap-thing now, and none of these guys is going to wait—probably have already ended the wait—and the recruiter thinks it's OK, so why am I so stuck on following some-thing written in a book two thousand years ago?

Maybe there was one other guy who was feeling like me and didn't want to go in, didn't want to know what he'd do when given the chance to stick a tip down a girl's shirt, didn't want to think about what girlfriend, Mom, and God would say if they knew where he was. So how come he didn't speak up? Why have I got to feel guilty when he didn't speak up either?

(Speaking to God.)

Why have you got to make the rules so strict? Why has the wait got to be so long? Why can't Debbie understand that I still love her, that I'm gonna hold out? The biggest problem is now they'll expect me to go again. And four months from now when we're going through basic to-gether and these guys are pulling my butt through mud and showing me how to load a grenade launcher, you think I want them to think I'm a wimp?

(Pause.)

I know. That's already been proven.

KISS ME
By Ric Averill

(TRISH is at a sleepover with several of her girlfriends, all of whom are talking about who's weird, who's in love, who might be in love. It is here that she reveals her thoughts about "camp boy.")

Trish

I think he whispered, "kiss me."

It was just the shortest moment when he passed me in the hall. I keep thinking maybe I misheard. Maybe he was asking, "miss me?" The thing is, I haven't seen him since camp, and when we were there all he did was dunk me in the pool just about every day—and then he wouldn't speak to me, especially if he was with his friends.

He e-mailed me, but just forwards of stupid jokes or games or stuff about his family and his dog and not really anything. I e-mailed back for a while, but fifty miles is a long ways away and finally I told him a lie—that I was getting a new e-mail account and then I didn't reply any-more and finally he quit writing.

Nobody would just say "kiss me."

Maybe he was hissing at me and I just heard what I wanted to hear, except I don't think that's what I want to hear from him. I mean, it was two summers ago and he was a whole lot shorter and completely annoying—*and* he has this weird, I don't know, zit or something, or like it was a zit, but now it's a sort of a hole in his skin, like those pictures in history of someone who had smallpox. Only it's not that big, and I feel totally shallow to even notice it, but it's just in front of his ear. Maybe if he grew sideburns, I mean, when he can.

My uncle grew sideburns because he does an Elvis impression. A really, really bad Elvis impression. An "I need to crawl under this chair until my uncle *stops*" Elvis impression. I wonder if camp boy does Elvis impressions. That's what Cheryl calls him—"camp boy." "Did camp boy say anything to you today?" "So are you going to kiss camp boy?"

Why would I kiss him? I don't even really know him.

Sometimes his hair is greasy—I mean, I don't know how you get your hair to look like that. I don't know if he just doesn't wash it or if he actually puts something in it that makes it that way, thinking that if he does that it will somehow give him a "bedhead" look that's supposed to be hot.

"Kiss me."

There's no way he said that. No one just walks down the hall, slows down and locks eyes with you and gets that kind of dreamy look and says "Kiss me." No one. Do they? I don't even know if he's smart. He came out of Anderson's class, and that's like, Directed Studies, which is where you go if you're not getting it. Wait—I don't mean, like, not getting *it*! I mean, like not passing English or history or something.

"Kiss me."

Maybe he meant "diss me" 'cause I haven't really admitted that I remember him from camp that year, like when he threw me that candy bar from the top of a tree and I hadn't even known he was there—all acting like maybe he was Peter Pan and he'd flown to the top and I was Wendy or something. Just thinking about it irritates me. Really. OK. I know what I'll do. I'll figure out if that's what he really said. When I walk by him today, I'm going to say...

"When?"

SATURDAYS WITH DAD...NOT!
By Kay Rhoads

(ALEX [or ALEXANDRA] discovers his mother preparing a "Welcome Home" dinner for his father, whom ALEX has never seen, and who is coming for dinner after being released from prison.)

Alex

Oh, I get it. This is that ancient film, *Guess Who's Coming to Dinner?* with Katharine what's her name and the black guy. The unexpected guest. Well, you can take one plate off the table. For good, Mom. My plate. Because I will not just move over and make room for...for...some man I don't know, don't want to know and would never even speak to if I met him on the street. My God. I don't believe this...Mother! You actually think we are going to, what...sit down and have some kind of family thing?

(With heavy sarcasm.)

"So, you just got out of prison today? Hey, Dad, that sounds great. How was it?" Well, not me. He's a convict, Mother! I don't know this man. I've never believed it, really. Not for one minute did I ever really believe that my father was in prison. My father died in a mountain-climbing expedition. Mount Kilimanjaro. It was in my fourth-grade geography book, this little black speck on the picture of a mountain. My teacher said it was just a piece of rock jutting through the snow. It could have been him.

The whole class laughed.

Oh, yeah. Then I turned ten. Ten years old. Too old to be-lieve in Santa Claus. So, what was I supposed to say, Mom, when someone asked? "Oh, Dad?, well, he offed someone but you know really he's just your basic guy-next-door type throwing the ball around with his kid and washing the car on Saturdays." *Saturdays*, Mom, all those Saturdays. Ah, but of course, it's more complicated than that, there were *circumstances.*

Hey, I got it, I'll call all my friends and have them come over and meet Dad who, due to complicated circum-stances, has never been home a Saturday in my life! "Sa-rah, meet my father. You know...the mountain climber? The one I said died on Mount Kilimanjaro? It's a miracle. He's only been away, studying, you know, the circum-stances of the formation of rocks and how to break them." "Jake, meet my dad. He's been captivated by, you know, circumstances, for something like the last sixteen years, my whole life come to think of it, and now he's coming for dinner!" Here? Tonight?

(Beat.)

He's not, is he, Mom? Tell me he's not. Like in our house. He's not *home*, is he? Or going to be, I mean, when he shows up...ever...going to be *home?*

YOUR BLISS AND HOW TO FOLLOW IT
By Tammy Ryan

(Her mother's recent disappearance has upset and confused MORGAN, who attempts to focus her energies on completing a college application form.)

Morgan

My mother has run away from home. She said she'd be gone three days; it's been a week. My father is in deep denial. But as weird as that is, I totally realize it's their drama. I've got my own. I had to write this boring essay for my college applications, which I told my mother no one was ever going to read, but that she kept nagging at me to do. So I put down all of my hopes and dreams for the future, you know: I want world peace, equality for women, political freedom for all.

Words. Right?

Nobody pays attention to words. If nobody reads them, they have absolutely *no effect.* So I decided from now on I am going for *action.* I am going to *do. Something.* I'm not sure what yet. But it will be something *big.* I found a great Web site: "Your Bliss and How to Follow It" designed to help you discover your destiny.

Okay, so I found out I don't belong in Pittsburgh. I'm more suited to the Pacific Northwest. Like Seattle or Tibet. I took the survey and it said I should be an environmental terrorist or a Buddhist nun. Either you are on your path to your bliss or you are totally *not*. It's a question of *when* I want to get on the path. I could finish senior year, or I can leave tomorrow. One thing I can tell you is I'm not gonna be like my mother and wait forty years before I follow my heart's desire.

(Beat.)

Okay, so as soon as she left I was inspired to rewrite my essay.

(Pulls out crumpled-up paper.)

Don't panic. This is just my draft.

(Reads.)

To Whom It May Concern. While attempting to write this essay I have come to realize the impossibility of explaining myself to a group of strangers who will make a decision about me that will change my life forever. Since I am giving you the awesome responsibility to alter my destiny, by opening or closing the door that could lead me toward or away from the person I was meant to be, I have a right to know who you are, beyond the course catalog and college brochures. As the customer in this exchange, after all, I ask you to respond in essay form to my seven questions:

Number One: How are you going to help me reach my destiny? Two: Keep my dreams alive? Three: Teach me to appreciate the now? Four: Live in harmony with the earth? Five: Love my fellow human? Six: Pass on what I've learned to the next generation? and Seven: Prepare my soul to die? *(Beat.)* Organize your answers in a carefully thought-out and well-written essay. You can be sure that your essay will be critical in my decision-making process.

(Beat, refolds paper.)

I think my parents' current crisis is going to help me find my bliss. I mean, I'm not happy about my mother leaving, and I don't want their marriage to break up or anything, but it's like she showed me the way.

Everything is suddenly crystal clear.

SKY'S THE LIMIT
By Kristina M. Schramm

(LUKE [or LUCINDA] stands before a headstone in a cemetery.)

Luke

Hey. It's me. Long time no see... Well, this is pretty weird...not exactly what I imagined. Somehow I thought I'd feel, you know, sad or something. But I just feel, I don't know, kind of stupid standing here talking to a...I mean, are you even in there anymore? Ashes to ashes and dust to dust, right? I remember that from your funeral. You know, all these years I've had these conversations with you in my head right before I go to sleep. But now I'm standing here and...

I mean I can't exactly ask you what you've been up to, can I? So, I guess we'll start with me. Well, first of all— just in case you can't see me—I'm a lot bigger than the last time you saw me. Of course I was only seven so you'd have to figure I got bigger, right? I'm in high school now...well not right now. It's summer here at the moment. Anyway, you probably want to know about school, so, let's see. I had AP Psych last year. That stands for *advanced placement*—which basically just means lots of homework. But it was pretty interesting. And the new history teacher, Mr. Dunlap? He wasn't bad, either. Otherwise, it was mostly pretty boring. Oh, yeah! I had *old lady* Clovis for English. Isn't that what you used to call her?

She's like a hundred now and everybody's still afraid of her. When she found out I was quitting school, she totally went off on...

Yeah, well, I've decided I'm not going back in the fall.

I'm in this band now. Danny—he's the bass player—he made up this sound he calls *Egyptian rock*. It's awesome. Nobody is doing anything like it. We call ourselves *The Pharaohs*. Get it? Yeah, well, Danny's cool. He's been in a couple of different bands so he knows everybody. He's gotten us some gigs around town and people are starting to take notice. Which is cool, but scary too, you know? Yeah, I still get scared every time I get up there. But once I start playing and people are like looking up at me...it feels...it makes me feel like I'm *somebody,* you know?

It sounds lame, but you understand what I mean, don't you? I tried to explain it to Mom, but she totally doesn't get it. She says it's a phase. A phase! I finally find something that I care about and she's waiting for me to get over it! Well, I don't want to get over it! It's like impossible to talk to her anymore. And then Dean puts in his two cents and... Oh, yeah, I didn't tell you. Mom's not with Dave anymore. He split a while back. Dean's the new guy. He's the one says Danny's a bad influence...and she listens to him! It's like she can't make a decision without him. She's never even heard us play 'cause Dean doesn't dig rock! What's up with that? Anyway, I haven't been home in a while.

Hey, I'm not on the street or anything.

I'm staying at Danny's until we leave. Yep! I'm going on the road with *The Pharaohs*. Can you believe it? I love saying that. Me on the road with a rock band! Anyway, I have to cut this short. Danny'll be here any minute so I have to go. I'm sorry I didn't come here before. I wanted to, but...

There is one thing...

Remember that night you took me to the carnival right before you and Mom split up? We went up on the Ferris wheel and saw all the city lights. And then we ate all that cotton candy and played that game with the darts? I wanted one of those stuffed camels so bad I started crying. Remember? But you didn't get mad. You didn't take me home. You just smiled and said, "You can never tell how things will turn out. Sky's the limit, kiddo, sky's the limit." Then you kept right on throwing those darts until the park closed. It didn't matter that I never got that stupid camel. It was like the best night of my life. And I just wanted you to know that now, whenever I get scared, I think about what you said.

Sky's the limit, Daddy. Goodbye.

WE'RE COMING
By Mike Thomas

(JACKIE, 15, is tired of being stereotyped. Not quite a full-fledged Goth and too independent to join a group, JACKIE just wants to be accepted as is.)

Jackie

We are a society of drug takers. The TV says if something's wrong, "Take a Pill." And we do it. My mom does it. My six-year-old brother does it. From Ritalin to Zoloft to…Viagra. Drugs are a part of our American culture. Dad gets home at 6:15. By 6:30 he has his tie off and a Jack and Coke in his hand. He says, "That's what my dad did," and he's been doing it since I could walk. He even taught me how to make 'em for him…

(Demonstrates with two horizontal fingers.)

three fingers high. Mom has about four or five different brown-colored prescription bottles she carries with her all the time. Her nerve medicine she says. Her Baptist upbringing would never allow her to touch alcohol. But I'm the crazy one 'cause I like to draw a spider web on my face from time to time and show people who I am? So if I look different to you or I have a piercing or I decide to paint black around my eyes then it must mean I'm on drugs. If you can't explain it, it must be drugs. Well, I'm not. You can test me right now if you want. I don't do drugs because they make you stupid and weak, and weak is one thing I'm not.

I've got three friends who self-mutilate. Yeah, they cut themselves until they bleed...for attention and a little understanding from...their parents I guess. They don't do drugs though. They say drugs will mess up your body, but slicing yourself with a razor is gentle care I guess? *(Beat.)* I tried it once, it's hard to puncture skin when you don't really want to. My heart just wasn't in it. It's not for me.

I want to belong to some kind of group but I don't...fully get along with any of 'em. They're all a bunch of hypocrites, if you ask me.
    (With sarcasm.)
"Don't do drugs!" What's that all about!! I know what... I'll start my own group...the Anti-Hypocrisy Group. And we can call America on its hypocrisy and arrogance for once. I'm in. Are you? America, hold on. We're coming.
    (A little laugh.)
We are definitely coming, with pierced eyes, tattoos and trench coats. Society, open up your doors 'cause here we come! And you're gonna be so confused 'cause we're all different even if we look the same 'cause that's just who we are.

Are you ready?

BALD

By Cynthia Mercati

(As she begins speaking, CHRISTY touches the colorful scarf wound around her head.)

Christy

"Grow it back," that's what Annie told me. That's the last thing my best friend ever said to me. "Grow it back." And I will. But just for now, just for a little while, I'm keeping it this way. I mean, I'm *not* keeping it. To keep her around, just a little longer.

Annie and I did everything together. First bra, first crush, first time shaving our legs. When I got my first glasses, horrible things with big thick lenses, Annie went to Wal-Mart and bought a pair of glasses just like mine. Then she poked out the lenses, so she could see. She wore those glasses every day.
(A beat.)
We were in the lunchroom when she told me.

We ate lunch together every day. Every day it was the same thing. Rush through the line, get to the table, set down my tray—and tell Annie about my morning. And listen about her morning. And feel better, just because she was there. Only that day was different, the day she told me she had cancer.

For a minute, the whole world went out of focus. The noise, the kids, the stupid Tater Tots someone had spilled on the floor, everything rushed together and got fuzzy. And washed over me, like the waves in the ocean. For a minute, I thought I was going to drown. And Annie wouldn't be there to save me.

(Beat.)

Then it all went back into place. Except nothing ever really went back to the way it was.

I hated watching her go through all the cancer stuff. Every other bad thing that had ever happened to us—the time she had to put her dog to sleep, algebra—we did it together. But the pain, and the chemo—she had to go through that alone.

So that's why I did it. That's why I shaved my head.

Annie told me in the hospital she wasn't going to wear a wig or a hat or anything when she got back to school. "People will just have to take me like I am. Bald as a plucked chicken." That's what she said, and that's how it was.

I couldn't wait for lunch, her first day back. I rushed through the line, sat down—and pulled off my scarf. And there we were, two plucked chickens. Together.

(Beat.)

"Grow it back," that's what Annie said to me on our last day—that last hour, when all that was left of her, was her spirit.

And I will. But just for now, just for a little while, I'm keeping it this way.

QUIET CHAOS
By Kevin M. Lottes

(TONY is at a rock concert. The crowd is going crazy over something happening on stage. Everyone is screaming at the band members, but not TONY. His eyes are transfixed on a very attractive young girl sitting alone, curled up in her chair, writing, not paying any attention to the band either. During the roar of the crowd, TONY takes this safe opportunity to tell her what is on his mind since she can't hear him anyway.)

Tony

I'm watching you right now, scribbling something with your fisted hand across the page. To whom you're writing a letter is unclear at this point, but you do it so softly. I'm assuming it's to someone very important to you, someone very special. Am I special to you? Just noticing you like this, while I stand here, in awe, over your quiet chaos. Even when you stop and close your eyes like that, to get the image back, you still hold my attention somehow. I just can't keep my eyes off you.

Even when you lean back in your seat and look down at what you've written, I'm thrown into something else with only the hope that you'd turn around and give me your eyes—just once. There you go again, throwing your hair back with that quiet whiplash over to the side. It goes up and over, out of your eyes, and I wonder how could something so quiet bring forth so much chaos rocketing inside of me? In spite of all these questions racing in my mind that I may never ask out loud, you continue to write away as if I wasn't even here.

Who are you writing to?

I'm here, yet you prefer to keep your back to me. That's fine and dandy, but you must understand something. I'll wait right here for you, forever if I have to, until you turn around and look at me! Because no matter how incredibly crazy this all seems right now, I assure you, you're the only quiet thing in this moment.

FORGIVING THE DEVIL
By Mike Thomas

(WILL, 17, has been caught drinking with friends twice, once by police, once by parents. He has agreed to talk to a rather non-conventional therapist, an ex-prisoner. The therapist has just posed a question.)

Will

Why does it always have to be a puzzle with you? Just tell me what I'm supposed to do and I'll either do it or I won't. "Forgive the devil"? Is that what you said? What does getting caught with a little beer have to do with the Prince of Darkness?

(He tries saying it different ways.)
Forgive the devil? Forgive the *devil.*

Okay sure.

Whatever you say, Mr. Druggie Ex-con Turned Social Worker, I forgive. Is that good enough for you? I feel "fixed." Isn't "Forgive the devil" a line from some heavy-metal Goth song where they talk about going to hell? You like to play head games to mess with people. Like…"Humans make mistakes, just don't let the mistakes make you."

(Sarcastically.)
That one is brilliant.

(With anger.)

You keep tellin' me no one is all good and no one is all bad, that the world is not that black and white. I don't know about you but I was taught the devil represents dark, black, evil and God, pure, white light? Right? Opposites, right? Isn't that what we are told at an early age? Do I have to forgive Jesus, too? What am I missin' here? They pay you for this kinda crap? Wow! I want your job.

(In a rush of pent-up frustration.)

I tell you I feel like my life is all confused, that I got two very different sides, not necessarily all good and all bad, but a kinda good and sometimes a kinda bad, and when I drink my two sides fight each other and you sit there and tell me I have to forgive some red-skinned guy with hooves on his feet and a pitchfork and a goatee? This is giving me a headache and you're full of it.

(Beat. His anger feeds this revelation.)

You mean me, don't you? Is that it? Ask me questions until I fall on my face? Hit me with every cliché in the... How fully do I have to forgive this devil person? Is it a full forgiveness? A complete forgiveness, down on my knees? Forgive him for what? Why should I forgive everyone that's ever hurt me, forgive all the people who messed up my life...and then forgive myself? Why? No one ever forgives me.

(Beat.)

Don't give me that, "I don't know" look. I am so tired of looking at your stupid face.

(Beat.)

We all have a little devil in us, don't we, Doc? Is that it? And it won't go away? And we have to "forgive" that part of ourselves first? Wow.

(He's still confused at applying this revelation.)

Oh man, that's easy. I so "got it." now. I do, I really do. A breakthrough and it's lunchtime and I've really... What do I have to do next, after I forgive myself?

What's next?

Hey, answer me!

YOU WANNA KNOW SOMETHING?
By Rosemary McLaughlin

(JUDY hurries on stage. She has interrupted a theatrical production. She addresses the audience, speaking rapidly.)

Judy

The show will be resuming in just a few moments. Hi there. Growing up I learned to talk very fast. I could get my father's attention if I started, "You wanna know something?" Usually, I'd be saying this as someone else at the dinner table was saying something, because someone else was always saying something. I'd wait for a break but there never seemed to be one. My family could talk like the Harlem Globetrotters, passing the conversational ball effortlessly from one end of the table to the other. I'd be exhausted, following them up and down the court.

I'd start asking, "You wanna know something? You wanna know something?" like I'm the Little Engine That Could, figuring some time, some *how*, some *one* would have to pause to take a breath or pick the pot roast from their teeth— "...know something? Wanna know something?" And then it would happen. Dad, blowing the whistle on my behalf, would say, "Yes?" and he'd turn to look at me and Uncle Fred would turn, and Aunt Mitzi and Ben and Allison and Mom would all turn and look at me and I'd tell them—
(Pause, then bursting out.)

"Nothing! I'm a moron! I forgot what I was going to say!"

(Sighs; long pause.)

That's why I learned to resort to—public spectacle.

(Up to the light booth.)

It's OK. Everything's under control!

(Resuming, speaking even faster.)

I wouldn't attempt it if there were fewer than twenty, thirty people at our house. I'd try the usual conversational opening gambits: "Did you know that all rodents, including rats and gerbils, have four really long incisor teeth in the front?"

(JUDY sees someone signaling from the back of the theater; to the audience.)

That's the director in the back. Hasn't she been doing a great job?

(JUDY claps, encouraging audience to do so; to director.)

They are not getting restless.

(Checks out audience; realizes they might be; talks faster.)

And when that wouldn't work, I'd clear away some chairs, yank up my skirt—they always made me wear a skirt—and at the top of my lungs I would do the cancan.

(Dances and sings.)

Tra-la-la-boom-zee-ay!
Tra-la-la-boom-zee-ay!
Tra-la-la-boom-zee-ay!
Tra-la-la-boom-zee-ay!

(Continues dancing, with more fervor.)

Then, I'd do it again, my legs pumping, my ruffled cotton underwear showing. And they'd go back to their conversation and I'd go and try to figure out why they didn't find me fascinating and then one time, it's my tenth birthday and I get really going like the genuine Follies Bergeres come for one night only to Bayonne, New Jersey.

(With more fervor.)

Everybody's watching me. They keep watching me. They can't help themselves! All my aunts, uncles, cousins, even my own family, and the only trouble is I've never had this much attention for longer than twenty seconds and I don't have a clue how to end it.

(Smiles too broadly.)

I'm smiling—

(Gasps.)

and dancing—

(Gasps.)

my heart out, trying to figure out what to do next, how to capitalize on all this attention, everything I ever wanted in my life and that's when my cousin Richie sticks a chair behind my legs and I collapse on the floor with a thud that registers 6.5 on the Richter scale.

(JUDY collapses on the floor. After a moment, she is physically removed from the stage—by a stage manager, another performer, even the classic "hook" might be employed. She struggles valiantly. As she is being removed from the stage.)

Wait!! The show will... This isn't how I thought my life was going to turn out! Wouldn't want you to think about me!

ABOUT THE PLAYWRIGHTS

DAVID ALEX has written a variety of award-winning plays including **A Slice of Teen Life: Monologues for Teens, By the Rivers of Babylon, The Lutwidge Canvass, Eroica, Ride of a Lifetime, The Tinker Wins** and **The E-Mail Conspiracy**. In 1999, **Ends** was an African-American Theatre Festival award winner; and in 2000, **Onto Infinity** won the Das Goldkiel Award. His works have been staged by New Jersey Repertory Company, Chicago Playwrights' Center and Bailiwick Repertory.

RIC AVERILL is the artistic director of the Seem-To-Be-Players as well as a playwright-musician whose works include, among others, **The Seven Voyages of Sinbad the Sailor; Bird Woman: The Story of Sacagawea; Pixies, Kings and Magical Things** and **Alex and the Shrink World**. He is a winner of the Distinguished Play award from the American Alliance for Theatre and Education, and a two-time participant in both The Kennedy Center's New Visions/New Voices and the Bonderman/IUPUI Youth Theatre Playwriting Symposium. He has received commissions from the Coterie Theatre, the Kansas Health Foundation and First Stage in Milwaukee. In 2003-2004, **The Emperor's New Clothes**, an opera for children commissioned by The Kennedy Center, toured extensively throughout the United States.

SANDRA FENICHEL ASHER has published over two dozen plays, including **Across the Plains: The Journey of the Palace Wagon Family, Emma, I Will Sing Life, In the Garden of the Selfish Giant, Somebody Catch My Homework** and **A Woman Called Truth** (all available from Dramatic Publishing). Her adaptation of Avi's **Romeo and Juliet Together (and Alive!) At Last**, co-commissioned by Laguna Playhouse Youth Theater and the University of Utah Theatre Department, premiered in 2003 at the Laguna Playhouse. The University of Utah Youth Theatre also performed the piece as part of The Kennedy Center Imagination Celebration season. She is the recipient of the Distinguished Play award from the American Alliance for Theatre and Education, and the American Alliance for Theatre and Education's Charlotte B. Chorpenning Playwright Award honoring a nationally known writer of outstanding plays for children. Asher is a member of The Dramatists Guild and co-founder of USA Plays for Kids.

MAX BUSH is a freelance playwright, director and screenwriter whose theatrical works have been commissioned by Nashville Academy Theatre, Lexington Children's Theatre, Honolulu Theatre for Youth, Karamu House, Hartford Children's Theatre and the Goodman/DePaul School of Drama. His works include, among others, **The Boy Who Left Home to Find Out About the Shivers, Chest of Dreams, Ezigbo, The Adventure of Treasure Island, Sarah, The Spirit Child, Emerald Circle** and **The Three Musketeers**. He has participated in the Bonderman/IUPUI Youth Theatre Playwriting Symposium, and is the recipient of the American Alliance for Theatre and Education's Charlotte B. Chorpenning Playwright Award honoring a nationally known writer of outstanding plays for children.

MARCIA CEBULSKA is an award-winning playwright whose works have been produced in New York City, Los

Angeles, Indianapolis, Chicago and elsewhere throughout the United States. In 1989, **And When the Bough Breaks** won the Jane Chambers Playwriting Award; and in 2001, **Visions of Right** won the Dorothy Silver Award. A three-time recipient of Master Artist Fellowships from the Indiana Arts Commission, Cebulska has been artist-in-residence at the University of Georgia, Marion College and the William Inge Center for the Arts. She is a member of The Dramatists Guild and Chicago Dramatists.

JOANNA LEIGH CONGALTON attends Rowan University in Glassboro, N.J., where she is majoring in Theatre Arts and English. While studying playwriting with Dr. Joseph Robinette, she wrote **Back of the Bus** and **Campaign Race**. Other works include a one-act play entitled **He Who Throws Stones** and over 200 poems, short stories and monologues. Congalton is the recipient of the Theatre Arts department's Newcomers Award, as well as awards for Best Stage Management and Lighting Design.

DOUG COONEY is a playwright, screenwriter and novelist who has been honored by the National Endowment for the Arts, the MacDowell Colony, the Lila-Wallace *Readers Digest* Fund and the MacArthur Foundation. His plays, among others, include **My Journey to Here and Now**, **A Forest for the Trees**, **The Final Tour**, **Johnnie Brown** and **Live Alligator Wrestling**. He collaborated with composer David O on the original youth musical, **The Legend of Alex**, and on the musical adaptation of George Saunders' **The Very Persistent Gappers of Frip**, which was developed at The Kennedy Center's New Visions/ New Voices in 2004. He has been commissioned by Mark Taper Forum, South Coast Repertory, Florida Stage,

Cincinnati Playhouse in the Park and Alabama Shakespeare Festival. Cooney is also the author of a series of books for young readers including *The Beloved Dearly, I Know Who Likes You* and *No Such Thing as Magic* (Simon and Schuster).

ELLEN FAIREY is a Chicago playwright, essayist and short-story writer whose plays, **Tuning in El Paso** and **Goodbye Pablo, Goodbye George**, were produced as part of the Collaboration Sketchbook Festival in 2000 and 2001. **The Kids Are Alright**, a collection of three short plays, is published on the Web by pulpbits.com. Fairey works in advertising and is also a freelance magazine and travel writer (bootsnall.com). She is a graduate of The School of Art Institute of Chicago.

NANCY GALL-CLAYTON is a Kentucky author who has written several award-winning plays. In 2002, **General Orders No. 11** won the Streisand Festival of New Jewish Plays award. In 2003, **The Colored Door at the Train Depot** was a finalist of the Southeastern Theatre Conference New Play Project, and **Felicity's Family Tree** won the Eileen Heckart Drama for Seniors competition, 10-minute division. Gall-Clayton has been a finalist three-time for the Actors Theatre of Louisville National Ten-Minute Play Contest and is the recipient of grants from the Kentucky Foundation for Women and the Kentucky Arts Council. She is a member of The Dramatists Guild.

CLAUDIA HAAS is a Minnesota artist-in-residence and the playwright-in-residence with Minnesota's Lakeshore Players whose works, including **The Tailor; Shakespeare**

Unbound; **Commedia Delight!** and **Anansi, the Clever Spider**, have been produced throughout the United States and South Africa. In 2001, **The Haunting of Will Shakespeare** won the Jackie White Memorial National Children's Playwriting Contest. Other honors include Nantucket Short Play Festival and Marilyn Hall Youth Theatre awards. She is published by I.E. Clark and Eldridge Publishing.

ELIZABETH HEMMERDINGER is a playwright and screenwriter whose stage works include **Fine Family**, **Chicopee**, **Squall**, **Star Dust**, **We Can Do It** and **The Rage Play Cycle**. Her plays been produced at Williamstown Theatre Festival, LaMama, and the Tiffany Theater in Los Angeles, among other venues. She is a 1998 winner of the Denver Center Theatre's US West TheatreFest, and the 2003 winner of the Speaking Ring Theatre's Vitality Playwriting Festival. In 2003, she earned an MFA in dramatic writing from the Tisch School of the Arts where she won the Harry Kondoleon Playwriting Prize.

KERRI KOCHANSKI is the producing director and a resident playwright with New Jersey Dramatists/The Waterfront Ensemble. Her plays, including **Counting the Days**, **Piece**, **Slice**, **Spitting Daisies**, **Seaglass**, **Communicating Through the Sunset** and **Stroke My Eyeball Butter Up My Lashes**, have been produced throughout the country and at numerous venues in New York City. In 1997, **The Question** and **Cup Is Cup** won an off-off Broadway Review award; and in 2004, **Penis Envy** was a finalist of the O'Neill Playwrights Conference. Her work is published in *New Plays Festival* (iUniverse.com) and *Young Women's Monologs from Contemporary Plays* (Meriwether Publishing). She holds an MFA in Playwriting from Columbia University and a Certificate in Film Production from New York University.

CHRISTA KREIMENDAHL is a Florida playwright whose plays, including **IM SM**, **Radio Head**, **What a Tangled Web** and **Black-eyed Jack**, have enjoyed readings and productions in south Florida at The Players Theatre and The Riverfront Theatre, as well as Funny...That Way! in Atlanta, Ga. In 2003, **First House of Neptune** was workshopped at Woodbridge International Playwrights Lab in St. Petersburg. She is presently working on an evening of monologues and a full-length play entitled **The Luna Cycle: or Bulldozing the Leftovers.**

ROBIN RICE LICHTIG is the author of over two dozen plays to include award winners **Embracing the Undertoad**, winner of Chicago's Bailiwick Rep Lesbian Theatre Initiative in 2002, and **Harmony**, winner of the 2002 Maxim Mazumdar competition at Alleyway Theatre in Buffalo, N.Y. Other plays include **Humans Remain**, presented during The Lark Theatre's 2003 Playwrights Week in New York City, and **Lola and the Planet of Glorious Diversity**, which was a Moondance International Film Festival finalist in 2003. Lichtig is a member of The Dramatists Guild, the International Centre for Women Playwrights, and Manhattan Oracles.

KEVIN M. LOTTES is a Network Playwright for the Chicago Dramatists. His plays, including **The Leash of the Rainbow's Meow**, **The Line Shack** and **Passing Red Dodges**, have been produced at the MadLab Theatre in Columbus, Ohio, and the University of Southern Indiana.

A freelance writer, Lottes' articles, "Arthur Miller: The Illuminator of Lunacy" and "The Greatest Album Covers That Never Were," have been published in *dialogue* magazine. His book of monologues, short stories and poems, *First Person Last*, is the debut release of his own Web site book-publishing company: barehanded books.

EDWARD MAST has written a variety of plays and solo performances that have been seen in New York City, Chicago, Seattle, Washington, D.C., Los Angeles and San Francisco, as well as in England, Israel and Palestine. His works include **The Million Bells of Ocean**, **Sahmatah** (co-written with Hanna Eady), **The War Prayer**, **Hidden Terrors: Tales from Edgar Allen Poe**, **The Tengu of Kami** and **Sundiata**, as well as adaptations of **An Enemy of the People** and **20,000 Leagues Under the Sea**.

LUCINDA MCDERMOTT is a playwright and performer whose works include **Betting On Serenity**, **Dear Vivian and Rachel** and **Feeding On Mulberry Leaves**, which won the Delaunney Prize in Playwrighting in 1997. Commissioned works include **Courage By the Sea**, for the Gibbes Museum of Art, Charleston, S.C.; **Inferno**, for the Chrysler Museum of Art, Norfolk, Va.; and **Rappin' Rapunzel** and **Lily y La Mariposa**, both for ChildsPlay at the Generic Theatre in Norfolk, Va. McDermott has studied acting at the HB Studios in New York City and is a member of Actors Equity Association and The Dramatists Guild.

ROSEMARY MCLAUGHLIN is a poet and playwright whose plays include **The Raw and the Cooked**, **Voices Carry**, **The Red Wagon** and **Standing in the Shadows**.

Her works have been widely produced in New York City, Chicago, Minneapolis, Sacramento and London. She has recently been commissioned by the Playwrights Theatre of New Jersey to write **Paterson Falls**, the first in a trilogy of plays about silk mills, salons and the birth of American Playwriting. A member of The Dramatists Guild, she received her MFA in playwriting from Rutgers University, and is associate professor of theatre arts at Drew University.

CYNTHIA MERCATI is a teacher, novelist and playwright-in-residence at the Des Moines Playhouse. Her works, including **Makin' It**, **The Strength of Their Spirit**, **The Baseball Show**, **Bigger Than Life** and **The Emperor's New Clothes**, have been produced throughout the United States. In 1999, **To See the Stars** was a winner of the Bonderman/IUPUI Youth Theatre Playwriting Symposium. She also is the author of several historical novels including *A Light in the Sky*, *The Secret Room*, *A Trip Through Time* and *Ya Gotta Have Goop!* (Perfection Learning).

MARK PLAISS is a playwright and writer who lives in La Porte, Ind. His work is featured in *Scenes and Monologues for Young Actors* and *Short Stuff: Ten- to Twenty-Minute Plays for Mature Actors* (Dramatic Publishing). In 1991, his book *The Road to Indianapolis: Inside a Season of Indiana High School Basketball* was published by Bonus Books. His most recent book, *The Inner Room: A Journey into Lay Monasticism* was published in 2002 by St. Anthony Messenger Press. A series of his essays are currently being serialized in the journal *Deacon Digest*.

JETT PARSLEY attended Duke University and received her MFA in Dramatic Writing from New York University. Her works include **Right Side Wrong, First Born, Hiss, Locked Doors and Lightning Bugs** and **Tar River Love Story**. She is published in *Scenes and Monologues for Young Actors* (Dramatic Publishing), *30 Ten-Minute Plays for 2 Actors* (Smith and Kraus). She has also written numerous scripts for churches in New York City and Chapel Hill, N.C.

KAY RHOADS spent much of her professional life as an administrator of programs and services at the Iowa Correctional Institution for Women in Mitchellville, Iowa. She is the author of **From the Backseat, The Stone Naked Woman, Prison of the Lost Souls** and **Caught in the Wake**. In 1999, **The Burning Pile**, a play about family abuse and the courage of a mother to stand up to her husband, premiered at the Alleyway Theatre in Buffalo. It was featured in 2000 at the Women Playwrights International Conference in Athens, Greece. She is published by Eldridge Publishing, HaveScripts.com and Smith and Kraus.

JULIA ROSE is a director and founding member of the Heartbreak Theater Company of Minneapolis, where she currently serves as administrative director. A student at New York University, she is the author of the plays **Fancy a Shag?** and **Italian Phrasebook**.

TAMMY RYAN is a four-time recipient of the Pennsylvania Council on the Arts Playwriting Fellowship, and the 1997 winner of the Pittsburgh Cultural Trust's Creative Achievement Award as Emerging Artist. Her works, including **Pig, In the Shape of a Woman, Dark Part of the Forest, Vegetable Love** and **The Boundary**, have been produced across the country. In 2004, **The Music Lesson**, developed at the Bonderman/IUPUI Youth Theatre Playwriting Symposium, won the Distinguished Play Award from the American Alliance for Theatre and Education. Ryan earned her MFA in playwriting from Carnegie-Mellon University and has taught playwriting at Point Park College, the Pittsburgh Playhouse and Rogers Middle School for the Performing Arts.

KRISTINA M. SCHRAMM is a performer and playwright whose works, including **Pirate Bones** and **Miss Fortune**, have been produced at Chicago's Lincoln Square Theater. An artist and designer by trade, she has designed the sets and costumes for a number of productions including **Angels in America** and **Beast on the Moon**. Her acting credits include **Lord Byron's Love Letters, Luv, Animal Farm** and **The Laramie Project**.

MIKE THOMAS is a southwest playwright, actor and educator who has performed as a stand-up comedian, and as a featured actor in several independent films. He has twice been nominated for Disney's Teacher of the Year Award. In 2004, he co-directed a seminar for teachers, sponsored by the University of Arkansas College of Education, to illustrate how dramatic writing can enrich their curricula. His writing is featured in *A Grand Entrance: Scenes and Monologues for Mature Actors* and *Scenes and Monologues for Young Actors* (Dramatic Publishing).

RACHEL FELDBIN URIST is a three-time recipient of the Individual Creative Artists Award from the Michigan

Council for the Arts, and winner of four national playwriting competitions including the John Gassner Memorial Playwriting Competition in 1983 and the FRS Drama Award in 1986. Her plays include, among others, **Shylock's Daughter, Thin Ice, Dear Jason, Clowns on Ice** and **The Talking Cure**. Urist is founder and executive director of New Voices, a non-profit organization whose mission is to promote self-discovery through theatre. She is published in *A Grand Entrance: Scenes and Monologues for Mature Actors* (Dramatic Publishing).

ELIZABETH WONG is a playwright whose plays, including **Punk Girls, China Doll, Badass of the RIP Eternal, Letters to a Student Revolutionary** and **Kimchee & Chitlins (A Serious Comedy About Getting Along)**, have been produced widely throughout the United States. She collaborated with Grammy-winning composer Michael Silversher on **The Happy Prince**, an opera for young audiences produced at the 2003 Prelude Festival in Washington, D.C. Her many commissions include Actors Theatre of Louisville, Cincinnati Playhouse in the Park, and Mark Taper Forum. She is currently writing **Ibong Adarna**, a play with songs commissioned by Honolulu Theatre for Youth, and an adaptation of **Goloshes of Fortune**, commissioned by Denver Center Theatre to commemorate the 200th birthday of Hans Christian Andersen. Wong is a former *Los Angeles Times* editorial columnist and a Disney Writers Fellow.

PERMISSION ACKNOWLEDGMENTS

ARE YOU WITH ME? by Marcia Cebulska. Copyright 2004. Printed by permission of the author. Excerpted from NOW LET ME FLY by Marcia Cebulska, copyright 2004. Inquiries should be addressed to Marcia Cebulska, 217 SW Woodlawn, Topeka KS 66606.

BACK OF THE BUS by Joanna Leigh Congalton. Copyright 2005. Printed by permission of the author. Inquiries should be addressed to Joanna Leigh Congalton, 400 Abbott Ave., Ridgefield NJ 07657.

BALD by Cynthia Mercati. Copyright 2005. Printed by permission of the author. Inquiries should be addressed to Cynthia Mercati, 721 20th St., Des Moines IA 50314.

BEST FRIENDS by Sandra Fenichel Asher. Copyright 2005. Printed by permission of the author. Inquiries should be addressed to Sandra Fenichel Asher, 328 Church St., Lancaster PA 17602.

BOXED IN by Rachel Feldbin Urist. Copyright 2005. Printed by permission of the author. Excerpted from THIN ICE by Rachel Feldbin Urist, copyright 1985. Inquiries should be addressed to Rachel Feldbin Urist, 310 Awixa, Ann Arbor MI 48104.

BRAIN FREEZE by Kerri Kochanski. Copyright 2005. Printed by permission of the author. Inquiries should be addressed to Kerri Kochanski, 308 Tallwoods Lane, Green Brook NJ 08812.

BRICKS by Lucinda McDermott. Copyright 2004. Printed by permission of the author. Inquiries should be addressed to Lucinda McDermott, 1815 Grove Ave., Radford VA 24141.

CAMPAIGN RACE by Joanna Leigh Congalton. Copyright 2005. Printed by permission of the author. Inquiries should be addressed to Joanna Leigh Congalton, 400 Abbott Ave., Ridgefield NJ 07657.

COMING TO by Rosemary McLaughlin. Copyright 2005. Printed by permission of the author. Excerpted from STANDING IN THE SHADOWS by Rosemary McLaughlin, copyright 1998. Inquiries should be addressed to Rosemary McLaughlin, Theatre Arts Dept., Drew University, Madison NJ 07940.

CONVERSATION IN FOUR-PART HARMONY by Jett Parsley. Copyright 2005. Printed by permission of the author. Inquiries should be addressed to Jett Parsley, 935 Havisham Court, Wake Forest NC 27587.

DESERT DREAMS by Ellen Fairey. Copyright 2004. Printed by permission of the author. Excerpted from TUNING IN EL PASO by Ellen Fairey, copyright 2000. Inquiries should be addressed to Ellen Fairey, 4617 N. Damen #1, Chicago IL 60625.

DON'T TELL by Kristina M. Schramm. Copyright 2005. Printed by permission of the author. Excerpted from PIRATE BONES by Kristina M. Schramm, copyright 1998. Inquiries should be addressed to Kristina M. Schramm, 2156 W. Giddings St., Chicago IL 60625.

FORGIVING THE DEVIL by Mike Thomas. Copyright 2005. Printed by permission of the author. Inquiries should be addressed to Mike Thomas, 106 N. Olive, Fayetteville AR 72701.

THE GOOD FIGHT by Claudia Haas. Copyright 2004. Printed by permission of the author. Inquiries should be addressed to Claudia Haas, 2372 Lakeridge Drive, White Bear Lake MN 55110.

GOTTA GET IT by Cynthia Mercati. Copyright 2005. Printed by permission of the author. Inquiries should be addressed to Cynthia Mercati, 721 20th St., Des Moines IA 50314.

GRANNIE'S DESTINATION by Robin Rice Lichtig. Copyright 2005. Printed by permission of the author. Excerpted from GRANNIE BIRD by Robin Rice Lichtig, copyright 2000. Inquiries should be addressed to Robin Rice Lichtig, 780 West End Ave. #6A, New York NY 10025.

THE GRETCHEN WORM by Max Bush. Copyright 2005. Printed by permission of the author. Excerpted from ANOTHER WAY OUT by Max Bush, copyright 2004. Inquiries should be addressed to Max Bush, 5372 132nd Ave., Hamilton MI 49419.

GRILLED CHEESE by Doug Cooney. Copyright 2005. Printed by permission of the author. Excerpted from MY JOURNEY FROM HERE TO NOW by Doug Cooney, copyright 2002. Inquiries should be addressed to Doug Cooney, P.O. Box 65066, Los Angeles CA 90065.

HANDS by Max Bush. Copyright 2005. Printed by permission of the author. Excerpted from ANOTHER WAY OUT by Max Bush, copyright 2004. Inquiries should be addressed to Max Bush, 5372 132nd Ave., Hamilton MI 49419.

HARLEY'S ART FARCE by Mark Plaiss. Copyright 2005. Printed by permission of the author. Inquiries should be addressed to Mark Plaiss, 4137 W. Andrea Drive, La Porte IN 46350.

HOPELESS by Julia Rose. Copyright 2003. Printed by permission of the author. Inquiries should be addressed to Julia Rose, 5133 Knox Ave. S., Minneapolis MN 55419.

I CHANGED MY MIND by Nancy Gall-Clayton. Copyright 2005. Printed by permission of the author. Inquiries should be addressed to Nancy Gall-Clayton, 1375 S. Second St., Louisville KY 40208-2303.

THE INFORMATION BOOTH by Lucinda McDermott. Copyright 2005. Printed by permission of the author. Inquiries should be addressed to Lucinda McDermott, 1815 Grove Ave., Radford VA 24141.

JENNY'S WISH by Mike Thomas. Copyright 2005. Printed by permission of the author. Inquiries should be addressed to Mike Thomas, 106 N. Olive, Fayetteville AR 72701.

KISS ME by Ric Averill. Copyright 2005. Printed by permission of the author. Inquiries should be addressed to Ric Averill, 2 Winona Ave., Lawrence KS 66046.

LIKE LIGHTING A CANDLE by Christa Kreimendahl. Copyright 2005. Printed by permission of the author. Inquiries should be addressed to Christa Kreimendahl, 13701 80th Ave. N., Seminole FL 33776.

THE MAKEOVER by Rosemary McLaughlin. Copyright 2005. Printed by permission of the author. Excerpted from MOTHERLESS CHILD by Rosemary McLaughlin, copyright 1992. Inquiries should be addressed to Rosemary McLaughlin, Theatre Arts Dept., Drew University, Madison NJ 07940.

THE MIRROR by Claudia Haas. Copyright 2004. Printed by permission of the author. Inquiries should be addressed to Claudia Haas, 2372 Lakeridge Drive, White Bear Lake MN 55110.

THE NEATNESS FACTOR by Nancy Gall-Clayton. Copyright 2005. Printed by permission of the author. Inquiries should be addressed to Nancy Gall-Clayton, 1375 S. Second St., Louisville KY 40208-2303.

NOT ON THIS EARTH by Kevin M. Lottes. Copyright 2005. Printed by permission of the author. Inquiries should be addressed to Kevin M. Lottes, 5751 Avenue Chateau Du Nord, Columbus OH 43229.

ONE MORE CHANCE by Mike Thomas. Copyright 2005. Printed by permission of the author. Inquiries should be addressed to Mike Thomas, 106 N. Olive, Fayetteville AR 72701.

PHEBE, FRIENDSHIP AND A FAT SUIT by Claudia Haas. Copyright 2004. Printed by permission of the author. Inquiries should be addressed to Claudia Haas, 2372 Lakeridge Drive, White Bear Lake MN 55110.

THE PIER GROUP by Elizabeth Hemmerdinger. Copyright 2002. Printed by permission of the author. Inquiries should be addressed to Patricia Crown, Coblence & Warner, 415 Madison Ave., New York NY 10017.

PIRATE GIRL by Ric Averill. Copyright 2005. Printed by permission of the author. Inquiries should be addressed to Ric Averill, 2 Winona Ave., Lawrence KS 66046.

PURITY by Jett Parsley. Copyright 2005. Printed by permission of the author. Inquiries should be addressed to Jett Parsley, 935 Havisham Court, Wake Forest NC 27587.

THE PURPOSE OF A KITCHEN by Tammy Ryan. Printed by permission of the author. Excerpted from A CONFLUENCE OF DREAMING by Tammy Ryan, copyright 2003. Inquiries should be addressed to Ron Gwiazda, Rosenstone/Wender, 38 E. 29th St., 10th Floor, New York NY 10016.

QUIET CHAOS by Kevin M. Lottes. Copyright 2005. Printed by permission of the author. Inquiries should be addressed to Kevin M. Lottes, 5751 Avenue Chateau Du Nord, Columbus OH 43229.

RIDING ON THE HEAD OF A DRAGON by Elizabeth Wong. Copyright 2005. Printed by permission of the author. Excerpted from INSIDE A RED ENVELOPE by Elizabeth Wong, copyright 1997. Inquiries should be addressed to Elizabeth Wong, 1860 S. Orange Ave., Monterey Park CA 91755.

RIPPER GIRL by Elizabeth Wong. Copyright 2005. Printed by permission of the author. Excerpted from DATING AND MATING IN MODERN TIMES by Elizabeth Wong, copyright 2002. Inquiries should be addressed to Elizabeth Wong, 1860 S. Orange Ave., Monterey Park CA 91755.

A ROSE IS A ROSE by David Alex. Copyright 2005. Printed by permission of the author. Inquiries should be addressed to David Alex, 1060 Warwick Circle N., Hoffman Estates IL 60194.

SAMANTHA'S PLIGHT by Mike Thomas. Copyright 2005. Printed by permission of the author. Inquiries should be addressed to Mike Thomas, 106 N. Olive, Fayetteville AR 72701.

SATURDAYS WITH DAD...NOT! by Kay Rhoads. Copyright 2005. Printed by permission of the author. Inquiries should be addressed to Kay Rhoads, 1118 NW Greenwood, Ankeny IA 50021.

SHAKESPEARE IN HOLLYWOOD by Claudia Haas. Copyright 2005. Printed by permission of the author. Inquiries should be addressed to Claudia Haas, 2372 Lakeridge Drive, White Bear Lake MN 55110.

SKY'S THE LIMIT by Kristina M. Schramm. Copyright 2005. Printed by permission of the author. Inquiries should be addressed to Kristina M. Schramm, 2156 W. Giddings St., Chicago IL 60625

SLEEPOVERS AND SERIAL KILLERS by Tammy Ryan. Printed by permission of the author. Excerpted from DARK PART OF THE FOREST by Tammy Ryan, copyright 2000. Inquiries should be addressed to Ron Gwiazda, Rosenstone/Wender, 38 E. 29th St., 10th Floor, New York NY 10016.

SPLIT ENDS by Kerri Kochanski. Copyright 2005. Printed by permission of the author. Excerpted from THE PINK PLAYS by Kerri Kochanski, copyright 2004. Inquiries should be addressed to Kerri Kochanski, 308 Tallwoods Lane, Green Brook NJ 08812.

THINKING ABOUT LINCOLN by Cynthia Mercati. Copyright 2005. Printed by permission of the author. Inquiries should be sent to Cynthia Mercati, 721 20th St., Des Moines IA 50314.

WAR by Mike Thomas. Copyright 2005. Printed by permission of the author. Inquiries should be addressed to Mike Thomas, 106 N. Olive, Fayetteville AR 72701.

WEDDING TALK by Edward Mast. Copyright 2005. Printed by permission of the author. Excerpted from THE TENGU OF KAMI by Edward Mast, copyright 2004. Inquiries should be addressed to Edward Mast, 4330 2nd Ave. NE, Seattle WA 98105.

WE'RE COMING by Mike Thomas. Copyright 2005. Printed by permission of the author. Inquiries should be addressed to Mike Thomas, 106 N. Olive, Fayetteville AR 72701.

WHAT YOU CRAVE by Rosemary McLaughlin. Copyright 2005. Printed by permission of the author. Excerpted from VOICES CARRY by Rosemary McLaughlin, copyright 2003. Inquiries should be addressed to Rosemary McLaughlin, Theatre Arts Dept., Drew University, Madison NJ 07940.

YOU WANNA KNOW SOMETHING? by Rosemary McLaughlin. Copyright 2005. Printed by permission of the author. Excerpted from CAN CAN by Rosemary McLaughlin, copyright 2002. Inquiries should be addressed to Rosemary McLaughlin, Theatre Arts Dept., Drew University, Madison NJ 07940.

YOUR BLISS AND HOW TO FOLLOW IT by Tammy Ryan. Printed by permission of the author. Excerpted from A CONFLUENCE OF DREAMING by Tammy Ryan, copyright 2003. Inquiries should be addressed to Ron Gwiazda, Rosenstone/Wender, 38 E. 29th St., 10th Floor, New York NY 10016.